D1571240

100 THINGS

You Don't Know About

NOVA SCOTIA

Sarah Sawler

NIMBUS
PUBLISHING
NIMBUS.CA

For Sebastien, who's always up for an adventure
no matter how often we get lost.

Nimbus Publishing Limited
3731 Mackintosh St, Halifax, NS, B3K 5A5
(902) 455-4286 nimbus.ca

Printed and bound in Canada
NB1170
Design: JVDW Designs

Library and Archives Canada Cataloguing in Publication

Sawler, Sarah, author
100 things you don't know about Nova Scotia / Sarah Sawler.

Includes bibliographical references.
Issued in print and electronic formats.
ISBN 978-1-77108-377-5 (paperback).—ISBN 978-1-77108-378-2 (html)

1. Nova Scotia—History—Miscellanea. 2. Nova Scotia—Miscellanea.
I. Title. II. Title: One hundred things you don't know about Nova Scotia.

FC2311.S38 2016   971.6002   C2015-908188-2
                                 C2015-908189-0

Canada Council   Conseil des arts
for the Arts   du Canada

Nimbus Publishing acknowledges the financial support for its publishing activities from the Government of Canada through the Canada Book Fund (CBF) and the Canada Council for the Arts, and from the Province of Nova Scotia. We are pleased to work in partnership with the Province of Nova Scotia to develop and promote our creative industries for the benefit of all Nova Scotians.

MIX
Paper from
responsible sources
FSC   FSC® C103113
www.fsc.org

Foreword

Brier Island, Nova Scotia, was a magical place to be a little kid. Two ferry rides from the mainland, it was home to one small fishing village and a population of about three hundred when I lived there in the early 1980s. Everyone knew everyone. You could never get very lost, or into too much trouble, without someone noticing. It was an ideal place for a free-range childhood.

In the summers, by about 9 A.M., my parents would toss me out of the house. "You're not sitting on the couch all day," Dad would say. "Go do something interesting." So, with instructions to be home by the time the streetlights came on, I'd get on my bike. Sometimes I'd have an entourage of friends and/or siblings. Other times I'd ride solo.

There was a lot to explore. There were beaches on the north side of the island where flotsam and jetsam washed up. Once I found what appeared to be an old artillery shell. My imagination took off. Had the Second World War come that close? Did Nazi submarines roam the Bay of Fundy?

Inland, there was a compact but dense stand of forest. One day my friends and I came across the tumbledown ruins of a house. We had few scant details of its history, but we used those to conflate wild tales of gangsters, feuds, and murder most foul.

One of my favourite finds was a small stone monument at the end of a winding coastal path. Perched on the headlands, it overlooked the roiling North Atlantic. At first I just liked the spot's wild and rugged scenery, but as I grew older and more curious, I read the inscription on the monument. It marked sailor Joshua Slocum's solo circumnavigation of the globe. I was gobsmacked. My little island had produced a real honest-to-God adventurer.

I've never forgotten that feeling of wonder, of amazement, of being so directly connected to history.

A couple of decades later, I was editor of *Halifax Magazine* and Sarah Sawler was one of our regular freelance writers. When she told me she wanted to write stories about Halifax's quirky history—the unknown stories, the tidbits that make history come alive for people—that feeling flooded back.

As I read her article, and the follow-ups it quickly triggered, I was transported. I was that eight-year-old boy again, clambering along the shore beachcombing for artifacts, scraping the moss off a mysterious old monument, peering into the ruins of an abandoned house. It was magic then, and it's magic now.

History is so much more than dates or treaties or elections or battles. It's the real-life moments, those stories and flashes of insight that connect who we are now to where we came from. Many people live their lives convinced that history is boring and irrelevant, but they're sadly mistaken. Our history is who we are. Nothing matters more. For a writer to make people understand that, in the way Sarah will with this book, is a great gift.

I could go on, but the fact is: I want to go read this book right now. Discoveries await.

Trevor J. Adams, editor, *Halifax Magazine*
July 2015

Preface

Although I've always been interested in history, particularly the slightly morbid, almost unbelievable kind, this book probably wouldn't exist if it weren't for a meeting with my *Halifax Magazine* editor, Trevor Adams, in early 2013. The office was still on Hollis Street at the time, and we were tossing story ideas around a table in their tiny kitchen when we hit on something. Fifty somethings, in fact.

The resulting article, a collection of one- or two-sentence facts called "50 Things You Don't Know About Halifax," was published in the July 2013 issue, and I don't think my editor or I had any idea how popular it would become. I certainly had fun writing it—for me, it doesn't get much better than ghost stories and pirate hangings—but I assumed it would appear in the magazine, attract a bit of buzz, and disappear again, the way most articles do.

This one didn't go away.

There were radio interviews and TV appearances, and a couple of fascinating coffee meetings with people whose relatives had appeared in the article. Then there were three more articles: "50 More Things You Don't Know About Halifax," "Another 50 Things You Don't Know About Halifax," and "40 Things You Don't Know About Bedford." But for me, one or two sentences per fact wasn't enough—I wanted room to tell the stories, to put the "things" in context, to explore some of the little-known facts that took place throughout the rest of Nova Scotia.

And it wouldn't have happened without help. I'd like to thank the people and organizations who shared their knowledge, archives, and stories, namely the Maritime Museum of the Atlantic; the reference department at the Spring Garden Road Memorial Public Library and later, the Halifax Central Library; researcher and photographer Albert Lee; the Halifax Municipal Archives; the Nova Scotia Archives; Doors Open Halifax;

Greater Halifax Partnerships; Paranormal Studies and Investigations Canada; CBC; writer Wanda Taylor; the National Gallery of Canada; Neptune Theatre; Halifax Regional Municipality; Peter L. Twohig's amazing blog, "Weird Shit in Historic Newspapers"; author Hélène Boudreau; The Canadian Encyclopedia; *The Mark News*; author Chris Benjamin; and author Jon Tattrie. Over the last couple of years, I've thumbed through pages and pages of books and clicked through pages and pages of websites, so if I've missed mentioning someone, I'm sincerely sorry.

I'd also like to thank the people who kept me sane throughout the process, especially my ever-supportive husband and children. I'm also thankful for the good advice and listening ears of Trevor Adams, Kat Kruger, Emily MacKinnon, and Tom Ryan. Thanks to my parents, for their encouragement and for instilling in me a borderline obsession with books, and my in-laws for their excellent supply of local history leads.

Finally, thank you to everyone who read and enjoyed "50 Things You Don't Know About Halifax" and all the other articles. I hope you enjoy this book just as much.

Sarah Sawler
June 2015

1

The Mi'kmaq in Nova Scotia crafted eastern North America's first written signposts about 13,000 years ago.

According to Mi'kmaw oral tradition, over 13,000 years ago a band of hunter-gatherers arrived at the foot of the Cobequid Mountains, a range that stretches all the way from Cumberland County to Pictou County. From there, the Mi'kmaq settled all over Nova Scotia but primarily in Debert, Blomidon, Kejimkujik, and the Mersey River.

Today, the Mi'kmaw hieroglyphs that were written all those centuries ago are considered to be the first written signs in eastern North America. The carvings were a critical part of life for the Mi'kmaq—they drew images onto birchbark to communicate with each other in the woods, to use as memory aides, and to record scenes of everyday life.

In fact, Mi'kmaq petroglyphs, images that serve the same purpose as hieroglyphs but are carved into smooth outcroppings of stone instead of other materials, are all over Nova Scotia. Kejimkujik National Park and National Historic Site in Caledonia boasts one of the largest collections of these ancient carvings in North America, with over five hundred individual petroglyphs.

These images tell us a lot about what life was like in Nova Scotia before the European settlers arrived. Based on traditional Algonquian shapes, the images depict men and women in detailed traditional clothing, as well as hunting expedition scenes. A number of the petroglyphs found in Nova Scotia show a canoe with raised sides and a small sail being used to hunt porpoises.

2

Citadel Hill and Georges Island were formed by glaciers 10,000 years ago.

The Quaternary Age, Earth's most recent 2.6 million years, has been pretty eventful. The planet has seen species come and go, it's been through multiple ice ages, and it's experienced the impact humans have made.

Throughout the Quaternary Age, dropping temperatures, lower sea levels, and ice sheets so large they cover most of the continent have marked new ice ages. When an ice age ends (the most recent one ended about 10,000 years ago), the opposite has always happened: the planet warms up, and sea levels rise as the glacial ice melts and retreats back towards the North and South Poles. The grinding weight of glaciers and erosion creates new rivers, reshapes mountains, and deposits huge piles of eroded rock and debris.

During the last ice age, much of Nova Scotia sat at the bottom of an enormous sheet of ice several kilometres thick. Glaciers moved, grinding the landscape, and when they melted, they deposited sediment made up of gravel, rocks, and sand called glacial till. In Nova Scotia, that till formed several thousand drumlins—hills that can be as high as fifty metres and several kilometres long.

Two of our most notable drumlins, Citadel Hill and Georges Island, were ideal for underground defense because of their natural makeup. Since they are soft drumlins (meaning they're made up of softer debris), they were easy to dig out, but their height still provided the necessary view for a good military defense.

3

A runic stone dating back to the early 1000s was unearthed in Yarmouth.

In the Yarmouth County Museum, there's a four hundred-pound stone inscribed with a thirteen-character message on display. Army surgeon Dr. Richard Fletcher found the stone in 1812 while walking across his property on the west side of Yarmouth Harbour. Shortly after the discovery, the stone fell under a considerable amount of scrutiny: archaeologist and university professor Sir Daniel Wilson was sent a facsimile and asked for his opinion, the Nova Scotia Historical Society had a look, and a couple of newspapers speculated about where the stone had come from. There was no shortage of ideas.

According to a 1982 report written by literary scholar Kenneth Webster, "Many conjectures have been made to account for the extraordinary inscription on the stone. It has been ascribed to everybody who could have been in Nova Scotia, from the Phoenicians to Bill Stumps."

The most popular theory is that the stone was inscribed and left behind by Vikings in the early 1000s. Some say that Leif Erikson, Norse explorer and son of Erik the Red, chiselled the message.

Attempts have been made to interpret the symbols, but none have been confirmed. Translations include "Hako's son spoke to his men," an interpretation made by Henry Phillips Jr., the secretary of the Numismatic and Antiquarian Society of Philadelphia, and "Leif to Eric raises [this monument]," a possibility put forward by Norwegian scholar Olaf Strandwold. But these translations are still disputed and the inscription remains a mystery, even today.

4

When Jacques Cartier found Sable Island in 1534, it was a walrus haven.

These days, Sable Island is best known for the wild horses that roam its shores. But over the past six hundred years, the island has also been home to plenty of other animals: cattle, foxes, and thousands of walruses.

Jacques Cartier first discovered vast herds of walrus on Cape Breton Island, the Magdalen Islands (also known as les Îles-de-la-Madeleine), and Sable Island in 1534. Some believe this enormous colony may have contained tens of thousands of walruses.

Unfortunately, the colony couldn't survive the hunters that continually raided the island throughout history.

In 1598, the Marquis de La Roche attempted to settle on Sable Island. The would-be settlers hunted the walrus for food and skins before giving up and going home in 1604—only to return to the island a few years later to set up a walrus fishery.

The walruses had a brief reprieve until 1633, when John Rose of Boston wrecked his ship, the *Mary and Jane*, on the shores of the island. According to Governor John Winthrop's journal, Rose reported seeing cattle, foxes, and "sea-horses." After Rose escaped the island, word of the wildlife spread, and English and French hunters converged on the island.

Sadly, the hunting didn't stop there. In 1642, the Boston Merchants' Expedition—the same group credited with bringing many of the horses to the island—left with four hundred walrus tusks. Walruses were last seen on the island in the 1800s; today, the only signs remaining are the walrus tusks that are sometimes uncovered by the wind.

5

加拿大最古老的村庄

Pubnico was founded in 1653 and is the oldest Canadian village still occupied by its founder's descendants.

In 1650, regiment captain Philippe Mius d'Entremont, his wife, Madeleine, and their daughter, Marguerite, came to Acadia with their friend and governor Charles de Saint-Étienne de la Tour. When he arrived, d'Entremont supported Saint-Étienne by taking on roles as lieutenant-major and commander of the king's troops.

A couple of years later he was rewarded—Saint-Étienne let him choose a place to settle—with the barony of Pobomcoup. It was a significant chunk of land that now incorporates the cluster of communities known as the Pubnicos. Pobomcoup was also only the second barony to be constituted in all of Canada.

Once they settled into their new home, Philippe and Madeleine had four more children—Philippe Jr., Madeleine Jr., Jacques, and Abraham. Philippe Senior couldn't stay long; he was quickly named attorney general of the king in Acadia and as a result, he was obligated to stay close to the governor. Nonetheless, his family continued to expand in Pubnico, and there are still plenty of d'Entremonts in Pubnico today.

6

The Sambro Island lighthouse has been haunted since the 1700s.

Rumour has it the Sambro Island lighthouse is haunted by the ghost of a young Scottish mariner named Alexander Alexander, who was stationed on the island as a member of the Royal Artillery in the 1700s. The Royal Artillery, for its part, was stationed there to answer signals from the ships entering the harbour.

One day Double Alex, as he's now known, was asked to go ashore to pick up rations, as well as the wages for all the military on the island. While he may or may not have picked up the rations, he definitely picked up the pay: while on the mainland, Double Alex wasted all the money on a two-week bender.

The Sambro Island lighthouse, circa 1901. (*Nova Scotia Archives*)

When he returned to Sambro without the payroll or rations, his commanding officer and fellow mariners were less than impressed. Sources vary on exactly what happened: Double Alex either hanged himself instead of facing charges, or his fellow mariners killed him for what he'd done. Most sources agree that Double Alex hanged himself.

Over the years, sources have reported seeing Double Alex in and around the lighthouse, walking through doors and throwing things around.

7 加拿大最古老的墓碑.

Here lyes Canada's oldest grave marker: October 1, 1720.

Take a walk through the Garrison Cemetery on the grounds of Fort Anne in Annapolis Royal, and you'll find Canada's oldest existing grave marker, a worn slate slab still faintly inscribed with the words

Here lyes ye Body of Bathiah Douglass wife
to Samuel Douglass who
Departed this Life, Octo
the 1st, 1720, in the 37th
Year of her Age.

Above the inscription there's an image of a cherubic winged head, a type of engraving often referred to as a "soul effigy." According to various sources, these winged heads were meant to remind the living of the inevitability of death and represent the soul's ascension to heaven. It is a softer version of the more macabre winged skulls that were popular grave marker decorations in the eighteenth century.

The headstone of Samuel Douglass's second wife, Rebecca Douglass, sits next to Bathiah's marker. Interestingly, Rebecca also died at thirty-seven and, based on the glowing inscription, Douglass liked her best:

Here lies the Body of Rebecca Douglass
Who died April 18th 1740
in the 37th year of her Age,
was endowed with virtue and piety,
Both a good wife and a tender mother.

These grave markers are important artifacts in a historically significant cemetery. Although the cemetery holds about two hundred English gravestones, there are actually about two thousand bodies buried on the land. Before the British took over Annapolis, it was actually an Acadian graveyard, but since the latter used wooden markers, those markers eventually rotted into non-existence.

8

Halifax's first murder happened on Brunswick Street in 1749.

Halifax was a rough city in its early years. Arguably the roughest area was Brunswick Street, which was called Barrack Street because of the North and South Barracks located at either end of the street. At the time, Barrack Street was also known as "Knock Him Down Street," since frequent fights and occasional murders happened there. According to Thomas B. Atkins's *History of Halifax City*, "No person of any character ventured to reside there, nearly all the buildings being occupied as brothels for the soldiers and sailors. The streets of this part of town presented continually the disgusting sight of abandoned females of the lowest class in a state of drunkenness, bare headed, without shoes, and in the most filthy and abominable condition."

On August 16, 1749, just two months after Halifax was founded, Brunswick Street became the scene of the city's first murder. A British sailor named Abraham Goodsides tossed an unknown insult at a French sailor named Peter Cartcel. Cartcel responded by stabbing and killing Goodsides and injuring two other men who tried to stop him.

Cartcel was tried and convicted within five days and hanged two days after that by Governor Cornwallis. The hanging was criticized as harsh, but when Cornwallis reported the punishment in a letter to the Duke of Bedford, he was congratulated for maintaining English law and setting an example to would-be ruffians.

Cornwallis's warning must have been ineffective, or Brunswick Street would never have earned its colourful nickname.

9

Canada's first divorce was inked on May 15, 1750.

H alifax wasn't even a year old when one of its residents filed for the first divorce in Canada. On May 15, 1750, the unfortunately named Lieutenant William Williams claimed that his wife, Amy Williams, had committed adultery, and asked the Nova Scotia Council for a divorce.

At the time, cases like this were typically tried in an ecclesiastical court, a tribunal established by religious authorities in order to settle a range of disputes from adultery to slander. Since Halifax was still extremely young, there was no ecclesiastical court in the area. So, despite the fact that marriage was still considered completely binding under English law, the council, made up of Governor Edward Cornwallis and a few army officers, agreed to hear the complaint.

For one day, the Nova Scotia Council became the Court of Marriage and Divorce and Lieutenant Williams, his wife, and a number of witnesses presented their versions of the story. The verdict was unanimous: Amy Williams was guilty of adultery.

But the court didn't stop with granting the divorce. They also decreed that, although Lieutenant Williams was free to remarry, Amy Williams was not allowed to marry again as long as the lieutenant was alive. To add insult to injury, she was also ordered to leave the province within ten days.

When English authorities caught wind of what had happened, though, everything changed. Angered that the Nova Scotia Council had overstepped its bounds and authorized something that wouldn't be legal in England for another one hundred years, they disallowed the ruling. Unfortunately, there doesn't seem to be any record of what happened to the couple after their divorce was reversed.

10

When settlers arrived in Lunenburg in 1753, they drew from a random lottery to find out where their land would be.

St. Paul's Anglican Church on Cumberland Street in Lunenburg was packed on May 21, 1753, when the latest settlers arrived to draw from a lottery for their promised piece of land.

In the early 1750s, about a century after the Acadians arrived in Lunenburg, a large number of German, Swiss, and French Protestants arrived in Nova Scotia. The exact number of immigrants varies from source to source—some reporting 1,453 and others reporting 2,460—but all were lured by a juicy promise from the provincial government: fifty acres of land for each household, plus extra land for eligible dependents. They were also promised the means needed to establish a livelihood, including a year's worth of provisions and farming tools.

After the European immigrants spent a couple of years in Halifax, the government decided to make good on at least part of their promise by sending the newcomers to Merligash Bay, about 120 kilometres southwest of Halifax. The government surveyed the land along and near the shores of Mahone Bay, Lunenburg Bay, and the LaHave River. After the survey, the Crown decided to distribute 516 thirty-acre lots among the new settlers. They determined who would receive which lot by writing the names of the lots on the back of playing cards. The settlers lined up to choose a random card, and when they flipped them over, they found out where they would live.

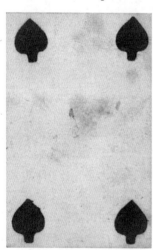

One of the original playing cards used in the land lottery, circa 1753. (Nova Scotia Archives)

In the 1760s, the Crown increased the land lots to three hundred acres, far exceeding the original fifty acres it had promised.

11

Slavery was common in Nova Scotia until the early 1800s.

When they think of slavery, most white Canadians point their fingers at our neighbours to the south. After all, the Underground Railroad led north.

Much of the history written about Nova Scotia in the 1780s perpetuates this misconception by emphasizing events like the arrival of 1,500 free Black Loyalists to Birchtown, Nova Scotia, in 1782, and minimizing (or omitting altogether) the fact that many of the British Loyalists who arrived here were slave owners; they brought their slaves with them to a new country. Some of the people already living in Nova Scotia had slaves as well. In fact, records show that between 1783 and 1784, the Maritime provinces saw an influx of about 1,200 slaves, most of them landing in Nova Scotia.

In this province, slaves were often called servants, but they were still enslaved—treated harshly and inhumanely. They're not to be confused with "indentured servants" who were offered employment contracts with the promise of a lump sum payment at the end of a set period of time. In the end, most indentured servants received no pay at all and were signed over to new "employers" without consent or discussion.

Slavery legally continued in Canada until August 1, 1834, when a British imperial act officially abolished slavery in the colonies.

12

Black Loyalists from Nova Scotia founded Sierra Leone's capital in 1792.

1792 was yet another difficult year for Birchtown's Black Loyalists, a group of people who had spent most of their lives being persecuted and enslaved.

The group of freed American slaves had settled in Birchtown, Nova Scotia, after the British promised to reward them for their loyalty with freedom and land following the American Revolutionary War. Although Nova Scotia was known as a safe place, it still had its share of social problems. Just one year after Birchtown was founded in 1783, the first recorded race riot took place in nearby Shelburne. Returning soldiers were having a hard time finding work—mainly because the province was experiencing hard economic times—and they blamed the Black Loyalists, who were willing to work for lower pay.

To make matters worse, the British hadn't made good on their promise of land and provisions. The hostile conditions and forgotten promises meant many Black Loyalists had to work as domestics and farmhands for very little (or no) pay.

In 1792, two men—a former slave named Thomas Peters and a British abolitionist named Granville Sharp—decided to work together to help the Black Loyalists resettle in Sierra Leone, Africa. That year, about 1,100 people left Nova Scotia with hope of finding a better life on a different continent. They named their new home Freetown.

Unfortunately, life wasn't much easier in Sierra Leone. A group of Black Londoners who resettled in the area had already experienced serious conflict with the area's indigenous people three years before the Black Loyalists even arrived. Within two years of their arrival, the French attacked, and about eight years after that, the area's indigenous people revolted again. Eventually there was peace, and today Freetown is the largest city in Sierra Leone.

SARAH SAWLER

13

Halifax was a busy printing hub in the late 1700s.

In an era when newspapers are regularly shutting down, laying off staff, and struggling to adapt to the new digital demands spurred by our universal reliance on the Internet, it's interesting that Halifax was once a significant player in Canada's news publishing world.

It all started in 1751, when Bartholomew Green Jr. arrived in Halifax from Massachusetts and set up a print shop on Grafton Street. As the grandson of the man who printed—and later edited—the first American newspaper, the *Boston News-Letter*, he brought generations of experience along with him. Green died just four months after he arrived and one of his former partners, John Bushell, took over where Green left off. The *Halifax Gazette*, Canada's very first newspaper, was born. The first copies were sold on March 23, 1752, and a version of the paper is still in circulation today as Nova Scotia's official government publication, *The Royal Gazette*.

In 1776, John Howe, another employee from the *Boston News-Letter*, arrived in Halifax. He brought with him a wooden printing press, and his business partner, the recently widowed Margaret Draper—Canada's first female printer. After a brief jaunt to Rhode Island, Howe returned to Halifax in 1780, set up a press in a house on the corner of Barrington and Sackville Streets, and published the first issue of his weekly newspaper, the *Halifax Journal*.

One December 13, 1804, his son, Joseph Howe, was born. He would eventually apprentice at the *Halifax Journal* and found *The*

Joseph Howe's iron printing press stands preserved in the foyer of the Nova Scotia Archives. (Joan Dawson)

Novascotian, which lives on today as a section in the Monday issue of the *Chronicle-Herald*.

This was just the beginning of a rich history of news publishing in Nova Scotia. Over the years, countless newspaper publishers have come and gone. At one point, the corner of Prince and Hollis Streets was constantly clattering with the sounds of printing presses—there were fourteen printing offices there at the same time.

14

Sarah Colley was Governor Wentworth's Halifax mistress during the 1790s.

On July 22, 1796, Halifax gained 543 new citizens. These were the Trelawny Maroons, a group of freedom fighters from Jamaica who had rebelled against their country's colonial government. After 140 years of struggle in their home country, the Trelawny Maroons were eventually deported by the Jamaican government and sent to Nova Scotia. When they arrived Sir John Wentworth, lieutenant governor of Nova Scotia at the time, was impressed, calling them "very peaceable, orderly, and extremely inoffensive." The Maroons were immediately hired to work on major projects, like the fortification of Citadel Hill, and invited to settle in Nova Scotia.

Most of the Maroons settled in Preston after a stint living in tents on Citadel Hill and in barns on Governor Wentworth's property, but one of the women who lived on Wentworth's property is of particular note: Sarah Colley. According to her great-great-granddaughter, Charlotte Colley, Sarah was both a seamstress and Wentworth's mistress. Their ongoing relationship resulted in a son, named George Wentworth Colley.

The Maroons weren't even in Nova Scotia for four years before trouble began. The details vary depending on the source, but one fact is consistent in all accounts: the Maroons were unhappy with their living situation, and the province was no longer happy with the Maroons. In 1800, the government ordered that the Maroons be sent to Sierra Leone, but Sarah Colley's descendants remain in Nova Scotia today.

15

In 1795, a teenager discovered one of Oak Island's most significant artifacts.

One of Oak Island's more interesting artifacts was discovered in 1795, when sixteen-year-old Daniel McGinnis was exploring the island. He came across a thirteen-foot-wide depression in the ground and, naturally, was curious. So he started digging and came back the next day with two friends: John Smith and Anthony Vaughan. After several weeks of digging, the boys encountered two platforms: one clay with visible pick marks, and one a layer of flat stones. After twenty-five feet, they needed more help. Since they were early settlers with heavy workloads, it was eight years before they were able to secure the funds and equipment to return.

When they did return in 1803, it was as part of the Onslow Company. This time, they had the necessary funding and equipment to conduct a proper dig. When they reached ninety feet, they found a flat stone that weighed 175 pounds, with a cipher engraved on it.

A replica of Oak Island's "cipher stone," which reportedly reads: "Forty feet below two million pounds are buried." (Ken Boehner)

Sometime in the early 1800s, John Smith, who had built a house on the island, incorporated the stone into his fireplace. The stone was removed in 1865 and displayed in the window of A. J. Creighton, a Halifax bookbinder. In 1919, the stone was still there, even after A. J. Creighton merged with another company. But sometime after that, the stone disappeared and hasn't been found since.

In 1866, a Dalhousie professor named James Leitchi deciphered the stone's message: "Forty feet below, two million pounds are buried." Joe Judge, a senior associate editor at *National Geographic*, later confirmed this translation.

Today, treasure hunters still consider the engraved stone an important clue, despite the fact that a researcher at IBM's Crypto Competency Centre thinks that the message is likely false. Either way, the missing stone is now an important piece of Nova Scotia history.

16

The ghost of a woman killed in a 1799 Sable Island shipwreck still roams the island.

In 1799, the *Francis* set sail for Halifax from London, England. The ship was carrying about 280 tons of cargo, including Prince Edward's books and household effects, several horses, and £11,000 worth of military equipment. She was also transporting more than two hundred passengers, including members of the 7th Fusiliers of London, an army surgeon named Dr. Copeland, his wife, child, and maidservant, members of the 16th Light Dragoons, and one of Prince Edward's household servants.

Unfortunately, everyone on the ship perished in December 1799, when it wrecked in a severe gale and washed ashore on Sable Island along with pieces of two other boats and the corpse of a woman. According to legend, salvagers cut one of the woman's fingers off in an effort to remove her wedding ring, and her ghost now roams the island, searching for its missing finger.

In May 1800, Lieutenant Scrambler, captain of the *H. M. Cutter Trepassey*, was sent to Sable Island to find out what happened to the *Francis* and pick up some animals. He did as he was asked and, according to a letter he wrote on May 17, 1800, he spoke to a few people while he was there, including the master of the *Dolphin*. The captain told Scrambler that he'd had two men posted on the island when the *Francis* wrecked. According to those men, when the woman's corpse washed ashore, they couldn't remove the ring and so, rather than cutting off her finger, they left the ring on and buried her body.

17

The first piracy trial in Canada took place in Halifax in 1809.

For thirty-five years, Point Pleasant Park's Black Rock Beach was one of the Royal Navy's favourite places to display pirate corpses. In fact, the body of the first pirate tried in Canada was tarred and strung up from chains inside a gibbet—an iron cage—on that very outcropping. Gibbets were common in the early 1800s, used as a warning to other pirates or mariners approaching the land.

The pirate was Edward Jordan, who also went by the name John Tremain. He was a passenger on board the schooner *Three Sisters*, along with his wife, Margaret, and their four children. They were travelling from Quebec to Italy, when, on September 13, 1809, Jordan assaulted the crew with a pistol and at least two axes, leaving two people dead. According to testimony from *Three Sisters* Captain John Stairs, Margaret Jordan also got involved, hitting Stairs several times over the head with a boat hook. After finding two of his crewmembers dead, the captain threw a hatch cover overboard and floated on the ocean until a passing fishing schooner picked him up a few hours later.

Shortly thereafter, a British warship found Jordan and the *Three Sisters* in Newfoundland. He and his wife were both tried on November 15, 1809. Margaret was found not guilty, possibly because of her testimony in which she stated that she was mistreated by her husband and coerced into helping him. Edward Jordan was found guilty and hanged on November 23 at Freshwater Bridge on Inglis Street. Officials moved his body to Black Rock Beach, where it stayed for almost twenty years, until 1844. A fragment of Jordan's skull is now part of the collection at the Maritime Museum of the Atlantic.

18

In 1816, a team of nine horses powered the Halifax–Dartmouth ferry.

Before the Angus L. Macdonald Bridge was built in 1955, people had no choice but to take the ferry if they wanted to cross Halifax Harbour.

The ferry's first incarnation was a large rowboat with sails and oars. When it was time to board, the ferryman would blow a conch shell and repeatedly shout, "Over! Over!" until he had a full load of passengers. Only then would he set off on the thirty-to-forty-minute journey across the harbour. The ferry was mutually beneficial for Halifax and Dartmouth, since Dartmouth provided Halifax with plenty of food and ice cut from its lakes.

The Halifax Steam Boat Company ferry service stepped up its game in 1816 and launched the team-boat: a vessel powered by a horse-driven paddlewheel that only took about twenty minutes to cross the harbour. The boat was similar to a catamaran—it was made up of two hulls connected by a platform—but the deck held something a little different: a horizontal cogwheel powered by the nine horses that walked in place on top of it.

Another option would have been to use a horse whim—a rotating cylinder with horses propelling long wooden poles that extended like spokes on a bicycle wheel—but this option often caused dizzy horses, so the service sprang for more up-to-date technology.

19

Joseph Howe accepted a pistol duel challenge in Point Pleasant Park in 1840.

It's never a good idea to insult someone's father, especially in print. In 1835, one year before he was elected to office, Joseph Howe published a series of letters in his newspaper, *The Novascotian*, accusing magistrates and police officers of stealing more than £30,000 from the "pockets of the poor and distressed" citizens of Nova Scotia over thirty years.

The letter was signed "The People," but the writer was a friend of Howe's, Mr. George Thompson. When Howe refused to publicly identify the writer, he was charged with libel and tried on March 2, 1835, by Chief Justice Brenton Halliburton. Howe represented himself and won, after providing extensive illustrations of how the people of Halifax had been swindled, and defending his right to publish the exposé.

But the controversy didn't end there. Five years later, in 1840, Howe published two letters criticizing the unnecessarily high salaries of Chief Justice Brenton Halliburton and Provincial Secretary Sir Rupert D. George, among others. He went on to suggest that these men could be easily replaced for less money and that their replacements would probably do a better job.

The chief justice's son, John Halliburton, took offense and challenged Howe to a pistol duel. In a letter to his sister, Howe explained that he felt he had to accept the challenge because, even though Halliburton was younger and had no one relying on him, he "had a right to make the demand."

The duel took place in Point Pleasant Park, near Martello Tower, on March 14, 1840. The men faced off and Halliburton took the first shot—but missed. Instead of responding in kind, Howe fired his pistol into the air and reportedly shouted, "Let the creature live!"

北美第一个动物园开放

20

North America's first zoo opened in Halifax in 1847.

O n Natal Day 1865, a thousand people strolled the paths, admired the plants, and ogled the animals of Down's Zoological Gardens: the first zoo established in North America.

Andrew Downs, a notable naturalist, ornithologist, and taxidermist, opened the zoo in 1847. It was situated on Halifax's Northwest Arm, close to where the Armdale Rotary is today.

Downs had the idea for the zoological gardens when he was still in his forties. In 1838, he proposed the project by circulating the plans, which showed infrastructure designed to accommodate a wide variety of animals, plants, and birds.

The only known photo of zookeeper Andrew Downs, taken in front of his aviary in Halifax, circa 1847. (Nova Scotia Archives)

Nine years later, Downs realized his dream. When it opened, the zoo spanned only five acres, but over the next fifteen or twenty years, it continued to grow until it sprawled across one hundred acres and boasted the largest collection of plants, animals, and birds outside of Europe.

In the 1860s, the zoo's growth coincided with a new interest in natural history—a trend that was likely prompted by the publication of Charles Darwin's *On the Origin of Species* in 1859. As a result, the zoo regularly attracted a parade of visitors—the Prince of Wales even visited in 1860.

But in 1868, while the zoo was still in its prime, Downs left for New York after he was recommended for a job as superintendent of the zoological collections of Central Park. On May 28, 1868, just before he left, he auctioned off the entire property, along with the animals and birds that called it home. The winning bid was between $8,000 and $10,000, and most of the zoo's contents were awarded to a Mr. Doull.

Although the information on the Central Park project is limited and differs slightly from source to source, it appears that Downs had some sort of disagreement with the park commissioner that resulted in Downs' resignation.

After his Central Park project failed, Downs came back to Halifax and tried to start a new zoological collection near his old site, but that project also failed (very possibly because it was so close to an existing zoological garden begun during Downs's absence, although this is speculation).

21

In 1848, a Pictou druggist was the first Canadian to administer chloroform.

Although chloroform has rather sinister connotations these days, in the nineteenth century it was commonly used for pain relief.

An American chemist named Samuel Guthrie stumbled upon the concoction in 1831 when he was trying to make a pesticide by mixing whiskey with chlorinated lime. Sixteen years later, in 1847, a doctor named Sir James Young Simpson decided to see if it could be used as an anesthetic—by trying it out on himself.

Despite concern about complications, chloroform quickly became a popular clinical anesthetic. Within a year, Simpson had administered the drug during childbirth in England.

On March 22, 1848, after hearing about the successful administration of the drug in England, a Pictou druggist named James Daniel Bain (J. D. B.) Fraser decided to administer chloroform to his wife, Christiana MacKay, while she was giving birth. To be fair, he did make sure that his mixture worked properly during at least two surgeries before experimenting on his wife.

Since the Presbyterian Church did not approve of painkillers during childbirth at the time, it's rumoured that Fraser endured lots of complaining and whispering before he either left town or was censured by the court of session of Prince Street Church in Pictou.

22

The manager of the Nova Scotia Telegraph Company helped lay the cable for the first transatlantic telegraph in 1858.

September 4, 1837, was a big day in communications history. That was the first day a message was sent by electric telegraph (using a line that ran from London, England, to Camden Town). It planted the seed for the first attempts at transatlantic communication.

Within a couple of years, the concept of the electric telegraph was already being tested—a cable was laid between Britain and France in the 1840s—and in 1850, Frederick Newton Gisborne began looking for a way to set up a submarine telegraph line that ran from Nova Scotia to Newfoundland.

Born in Lancashire, England, Gisborne settled in Nova Scotia after spending a few years in Quebec. He wasn't in Nova Scotia for long before he became a telegraph officer, then superintendent of telegraphs in Nova Scotia. He also created his own company in order to create the link from Nova Scotia to Newfoundland. The company folded early on, but he was able to pick his work up where he left off when he met Cyrus West Field, a businessman from New York.

Field had the connections needed to find the funding that Gisborne's idea needed. After consulting with Samuel Morse (of the Morse code) and oceanographer Matthew Maury, he created a new company called the New York, Newfoundland and London Telegraph Company—and made Gisborne chief engineer for a brief time. Gisborne left shortly after, but there's no solid explanation for why he left.

The company continued to make attempts at laying cable across the Atlantic after Gisborne left, beginning in 1857, but the cable broke twice. The project was put on hold for a year while they came up with a new plan.

When they tried a second time, in 1858, the line broke again.

But they were persistent, and they tried once more in 1858. This time, the cable didn't break, and on August 16, the first transatlantic message was sent from Queen Victoria to US President James Buchanan.

23

The Ovens was the site of an accidental murder in 1861.

On November 26, 1861, a group of men were gathered in a shop at the Ovens Natural Park on Nova Scotia's South Shore. One of the men, Reuben Tooker, was trying to sell the shopkeeper, known only as F. Traunweizer, a watch. According to a testimony from Tooker published in the *Morning Chronicle*, Traunweizer told him he had no money, but he *did* have something "very valuable." He pulled out a revolver, and all of the men went outside to try it out on a target that Tooker set up in the yard. The men decided to compete for drinks and took turns shooting at the target until they thought all of the bullets had been fired.

Just as the group started back inside, another man, George McDonald, arrived. According to Tooker's testimony, he heard Traunweizer call out, "Hello Mac; stand off!" Traunweizer brandished the revolver at McDonald, who responded with, "Fire away!"

Traunweizer, believing the gun to be empty, shot McDonald in the head, killing him instantly. According to witness testimony, "After the accident, Traunweizer showed so much emotion, I thought he would go crazy."

24

When Keith Hall was built in 1863, it included an underground tunnel connecting it to the Keith's brewery.

In 1863, when he was sixty-eight years old, Alexander Keith began construction of Keith Hall, his three-storey Hollis Street residence with an odd mishmash of architectural styles. While architect William Hay, who also worked on the Halifax Club and the railway department (now the Art Gallery of Nova Scotia in Halifax), drew heavily from the Renaissance Palazzo style, he also incorporated Baroque adornments and a sloping mansard roof. One source muses that the mix of styles is likely the result of a building plan inspired by both American and British building designs.

The Alex Keith & Son Brewery opened on Halifax's Lower Water Street in 1820. Here, a horse and carriage is loaded up for deliveries, circa 1871. (Nova Scotia Archives)

But Keith Hall had another element that's even more interesting than the mix of architectural styles: an underground tunnel connecting it to the brewery.

By the time Keith Hall was built, Keith had already achieved more than most people do in a lifetime—he'd served as mayor in 1843 (and again from 1853 to 1854), worked as a director at both the Halifax Fire Insurance Company and the Halifax Gas, Light, and Water Company, founded the Halifax Marine Insurance Association, and served on the board of the Colonial Life Assurance Company. He was also president of the legislative council from 1867 until his death in 1873.

Some people speculate Keith built the tunnel so he could keep a close eye on the brewery, while others think it was so he would have easy access to beer whenever he was entertaining. Either way, he built the tunnel because he wanted to stay close. Perhaps that's why people still sense his presence in some areas of the brewery today.

25

Victor Hugo's daughter, Adèle, lived in Halifax in 1863.

Adèle Hugo met a young man named Albert Pinson in Jersey, Channel Islands, in 1854. Pinson noticed Adèle reading by herself on a bench and introduced himself. The pair started spending time together, with Pinson sometimes coming for dinner at the Hugo household a few times a week. Within a couple of months, Pinson proposed—and was rejected.

Shortly after that, Pinson was sent to England with the military, but he and Adèle managed to stay in touch for a while. During that time, Adèle changed her mind about Pinson. She became infatuated and went to London with the intention of marrying him. When she arrived, however, she learned that Pinson had left for Halifax without telling her.

Not easily thwarted, Adèle snuck away to Halifax in 1863. When she arrived, she checked in to the Halifax Hotel on Hollis Street, registering as "Miss Lewly." Before long, she started boarding with local families—first the Saunders and then the Mottons. For the next couple of years, she stalked Pinson. She often wore disguises, dressing in men's clothing, or in all black. He continued to ignore her and, according to a letter from the Mottons to Adèle's brother, Adèle began to unravel—she started pacing her room and refused food and baths.

In May 1866, Pinson left Halifax for Barbados, and it wasn't long before Adèle followed him, to pick up where she'd left off. In Barbados, though, she traded in her disguises for rags. Adèle eventually received help from a woman named Madame Céline Alvarez Baa, who made arrangements for her to be sent back to her family in Paris. Upon her return to France in 1872, Adèle was admitted to a mental institution where she spent her time writing, playing the piano, and walking.

26

Alexander Graham Bell tried to save US president James Garfield from assassination in 1881.

Lots of people know Alexander Graham Bell, Nova Scotia's most famous scientist, invented the telephone. But only the most ardent fans of Alec Bell (and perhaps, the rare fan of American president James Garfield) know that after Charles Guiteau shot President Garfield at the Baltimore & Potomac Railroad Station in Washington on July 2, 1881, Bell was there, ready and willing to help.

Guiteau fired two shots: the first brushed Garfield's arm, the second hit somewhere just below his pancreas. The second bullet was the problem—it lodged in his body, and his physicians couldn't figure out exactly where it was, no matter how many times they jammed their fingers into his open wound.

Cue Alec Bell, who arrived at Garfield's bedside with a telephone and a device called an "induction balance." The idea was that the induction device would emit an audio frequency, and by connecting the device to the telephone, he'd be able to hear it. Bell thought that by running the apparatus over Garfield's body, the sound would change depending on how close the device was to the bullet, and they'd be able to pinpoint the bullet's location. Essentially, it was an early metal detector.

Unfortunately, Garfield was lying on a coil-spring mattress at the time, and all that metal completely foiled Bell's attempts to locate the bullet. The president died eleven weeks after being shot, on September 19, 1881.

The morbidly curious can still find President Garfield's spine, complete with bullet hole, at the National Museum of Health and Medicine in Washington, DC.

27

The world's best ice skates were produced in Dartmouth in the 1890s.

In 1864, a Halifax hardware salesman named John Starr opened Starr Manufacturing in Dartmouth. The manufacturing plant's original function was producing nails, but that all changed in 1888 when John Forbes patented the Acme Club skate—a steel spring skate that was a vast improvement over the block skates of the time. Block skates were awkward and hard to put on, and the new spring skates were easier to use, safer, and more durable.

Forbes quickly became the general manager at Starr Manufacturing, and his skates won gold medals at various North American and European exhibitions, including Paris, London, Chicago, and Philadelphia.

Although Starr Manufacturing's skates represented the biggest advance in skate technology in the nineteenth century, it wasn't long before the competition heated up. The company kept pace by frequently improving on their design, resulting in advanced products like the Silver King tube skate, which was favoured by the Boston Bruins until the late 1920s.

Unfortunately, Starr Manufacturing's skate department shut down in the 1930s, since hockey skates would have been considered a luxury during the Great Depression. The company itself lasted until 1996, producing the nuts, bolts, nails, and other steel products it was originally intended to manufacture.

- THE -

Starr Manufacturing Co.
(Limited.)

Works: Dartmouth, N. S.

Office: 74 Bedford Row, Halifax, N. S.

MANUFACTURERS OF

Cut Nails and Spikes, Wrought Ships' and R. R. Spikes, Machine Bolts, Track Bolts, Lag Screws, Square and Hexagon Nuts, Iron and Steel Set Screws, Washers, Boiler and Bridge Rivets.

Dies for Lobster and other Cans. Sheet Metal Punching. Difficult Machinery Repairs & General Machine Jobbing.

Ornamental Grill Work for Banks and Counting Houses. Electroplating in Gold, Silver and Nickel.

GENUINE ACME SKATES

THE STARR MF'G. CO. HALIFAX N.S. CANADA
SOLE MAKERS

Still ahead of all competitors. Adjustment simple, secure and effective. Workmanship and material of the best. Beware of imitations. The genuine only are stamped 'ACME.'

A newspaper ad for Starr Manufacturing, makers of the world's best ice skates, circa 1871. (Nova Scotia Archives)

加拿大第一个公共图书馆开放

28
Canada's first public library opened in Halifax in 1864.

Technically, the first library in Canada to allow public access was the Halifax Mechanics Library; members paid twenty shillings a year to access the collection that eventually boasted over three thousand volumes—an impressive collection for the time.

But those twenty-shilling membership fees weren't enough to sustain the library and in 1864, the doors of the Halifax Mechanics Library closed.

Fortunately, they didn't stay closed for long.

On February 19, 1864, the library issue was brought before council and with it, a proposal from the Honourable William Young. Young had purchased the entire collection and offered it to the city as a gift. He suggested council set up the library in an unused room of a public building, pay a librarian a modest salary, and open the doors to the public, free of charge. Council accepted the offer, which is good because according to Young's letter, "its rejection by the City Council, as representing the body of the citizens, would be a reproach to our public spirit and to our literary taste."

This new incarnation of the Halifax Mechanics Library became the Citizens' Free Library. Although this early public library system bears similarities to the ones we enjoy today, there were also significant differences. Some examples:

- No one under eighteen could use the library.
- Patrons had to pay a fee up front for borrowed books and were reimbursed when they returned them.
- Patrons could only borrow one book at a time.
- People visiting the city "for the purposes of literary or scientific investigation" could use the library as long as they signed "the Stranger's Book."

29

A peddler murdered on New Ross Road in the late 1860s still haunts the house he was killed in.

When mariner Cornelius Fader hired someone to build a home for him and his new wife, Novella Edith Webber, the couple probably dreamed of a cozy place to find refuge from the outdoors. Since the couple married in 1867, it's likely that the house, situated on the east side of the New Ross Road not far from Chester Basin, was built around the same time.

It seems that the Faders quickly developed a reputation for warm hospitality, because within a few years, their home became the kind of place that would welcome travelling peddlers.

One night, after welcoming a peddler to spend the night, the Faders went upstairs to their bedroom and the peddler went to sleep in the guest room downstairs. All seemed well until the next day, when the Faders went downstairs and found their overnight guest dead in his room. Apparently, someone had climbed through the peddler's window during the night and killed him. The murderer was never found and the peddler was buried in the Chester Cemetery.

But it seems that the peddler's ghost never found rest in its unmarked grave because, according to tales, the Fader house quickly became a poltergeist's playground. Locked doors swung open, empty fireplaces were mysteriously stocked, and groans echoed throughout the house. Before long, the Faders had had enough, and they abandoned the house and moved across the street.

30

The first set of standardized hockey rules was developed in Halifax in the 1870s.

The rules of hockey have evolved significantly over the last 150 years, but their roots trace back to the early 1800s. Although the birthplace of hockey is fiercely disputed, the Halifax–Dartmouth version of the game was developed in Dartmouth, when British soldiers and Mi'kmaw residents played an early version of the game together.

Colonel Byron Weston was one of those soldiers, and he recounted the "Halifax Rules" to *Halifax-Herald* sports reporter James Power, who published them in an article in 1937:

- The game is played with a block of wood for a puck
- The puck is not allowed to leave the ice
- The stones marking the place to score goals are placed on the ice, parallel to the sides of the ice surface
- There is to be no slashing
- There is to be no lifting the stick above the shoulder
- When a goal is scored, teams change ends
- Players must keep "on side" of the puck
- The "forward pass" is permitted
- All players play the entire game
- There is a no-replacement rule for penalized players
- The game is made up of two thirty-minute periods with a ten-minute break
- The goalkeeper must stand for the entire game
- Goals are decided by goal umpires, who stand at the goal mouth and ring a hand bell when a goal is scored

Although the Halifax Rules weren't published as such until 1937, they made their way outside of Nova Scotia when a Dalhousie-trained engineer brought them with him to Montreal when he moved in 1872. There, the Halifax Rules were adapted into the Montreal Rules, which were published in 1877 by a men's sports club called the Metropolitan Club.

31

The largest pre-*Titanic* marine disaster happened off Terence Bay in 1873 and was initially dismissed as an April Fool's joke.

It may not have its own James Cameron movie, but the story of the SS *Atlantic*, with its massive loss of life and negligent crew, deserves just as much attention as the *Titanic*.

Like the *Titanic*, the SS *Atlantic* was a state-of-the-art White Star Line ocean liner renowned for its unprecedented level of passenger comfort. It was built in Belfast, Northern Ireland, in 1870 and ferried 16,200 passengers from Europe to North America over its short lifetime.

On March 20, 1873, the ship left Liverpool, England, on its nineteenth voyage. There were about 950 people on board—including passengers and crewmembers—many of them immigrants looking forward to building new lives in New York. Everything was going well until Captain James A. Williams decided to stop in Halifax to refuel.

The captain was on the bridge until around midnight when he went to bed and ordered his crew to wake him up at 2:40 A.M. The crew failed to wake the captain, so no one took the usual soundings, no one manned the bridge, and no one watched for lighthouses. The ship drifted over twelve nautical miles off-course and at 3:15 A.M. on April 1, it crashed onto the rocks of Meagher's (now Mars) Island, near Lower Prospect and Terence Bay. The lifeboats were washed away, and only 371 of the passengers survived, despite the best efforts of the third officer and local fishermen, who hauled as many passengers as they could to shore.

When a group of survivors finally made their way to Halifax to report the SS *Atlantic*'s wreck and the number of fatalities, their tale was initially dismissed as an April Fool's joke.

32

A cyclone in 1873 killed six hundred Atlantic Canadians.

Hurricane Juan is still a hot topic among Nova Scotians, and probably will be for decades. Although Juan wreaked havoc on the region, a tropical cyclone that made landfall on August 25, 1873, cost much more.

The storm formed from a tropical wave in the Atlantic Ocean and made its way up the east coast of the United States. By August 23, it had reached Category 3 strength. When the storm swept across Cape Breton two days later, it brought gale-force winds and more than fifty millimetres of rain.

By the time it cleared, Nova Scotia had sustained 3.5 million dollars worth of damage, including the loss of 1,200 vessels, 900 buildings, and countless bridges and wharves. Around 500 Nova Scotians, mostly sailors, lost their lives that day and at least 100 were lost throughout the other Atlantic provinces.

Despite the huge losses, the storm did prompt an improvement in Canadian weather monitoring. At the time, Washington would send weather updates to Toronto, and Toronto would send warnings to the at-risk area. But when this storm knocked out the telegraph service, Toronto wasn't able to get through to Halifax in time to issue a warning. After the 1873 hurricane, politicians realized that they needed to improve the system.

33

The first sports organization in Halifax was the Red Cap Snowshoe Club, established in 1874.

In 1874, a new society was founded in Nova Scotia: The Red Cap Snowshoe Club. Originally made up of eleven male members, the club was formed in the hopes of promoting the sport of snowshoe racing. Based out of Coston House in Bedford, which was owned by one of the members, the club would often end up there to eat and drink after racing around the Bedford Basin.

The entire endeavor was quite successful. Eventually, between forty and fifty members were going on short "tramps" twice a week. Short-distance races, which ranged from 100 to 440 yards (or 91–204 metres), occurred about once a month. There were also long-distance races, but

Members of the Red Cap Snowshoe Club pose for a group shot in Halifax, circa 1885. (Musée McCord Museum Archives, N-0000.77)

they only occurred once every couple of years. The first one was a little over eleven kilometres long and took place in 1875, just one year after the Red Cap Snowshoe Club was established. They even had a rallying cry: "Are we or are we not?" to which the enthusiastic response was "We are!"

Red Cap member Sam Balcom from Port Dufferin was one of the original inductees into the Nova Scotia Sports Hall of Fame. Despite the fact that he'd only worn snowshoes three times before joining the Red Caps, he served as captain of the club eight times and won more than twenty races before retiring in 1939.

34

A robber used the visiting Barnum Circus as a cover to rob the Bank of Nova Scotia in 1876.

On July 31, 1876, the *Acadian Recorder* ran an ad with some big news: P. T. Barnum would be bringing "The Greatest Show on Earth" to Halifax. The ad stated that the circus would be in town for three days—August 1–3—and would feature "three monster special railroad trains," a "Noah-like menagerie," a "school of half-ton living sea lions," and "Barnum's $25,000 behemoth." After three days of parades in Halifax, the circus would be off to Truro and Amherst for more shows.

On August 1, the circus arrived as promised and paraded down Hollis Street, right past what was then the Bank of Nova Scotia's head office. The streets were packed with onlookers watching the spectacle pass by: an eager crowd that just happened to include most of the employees working at the bank that day.

Unfortunately, there was at least one person who was more interested in the bank than the parade. He was a man "of decent appearance" who got inside by knocking on the basement door, which was opened by either the wife of a clerk or a janitor—accounts vary on this point. He claimed to have dropped something important into a grate and asked if he could come in and get it. He was allowed in, and when the bank staff returned from the parade, they discovered more than $20,000 missing (reports vary on the exact amount). Although three men were arrested in Bedford in connection with the theft, no one was ever charged.

The advertisement for P. T. Barnum's famed "Travelling World's Fair" that ran in the Acadian Recorder *on July 31, 1876. (*Nova Scotia Archives*)

35

Oscar Wilde gave an art lecture in Halifax in 1882.

When Oscar Wilde visited Halifax in 1882, the art world was smack dab in the middle of the Aesthetic Movement, a controversial artistic movement that simply celebrated beauty and eschewed any underlying moral message, which ran counter to the Victorian sensibilities of the time. Critic Théophile Gautier dubbed it "art for art's sake."

Wilde's visit to Halifax was part of his North American lecture tour. He was such a staunch supporter of the Aesthetic Movement that its critics began to portray him as a bit of a caricature. Gilbert & Sullivan (librettist W. S. Gilbert and composer Arthur Sullivan) wrote a play called *Patience*, which opened in London on April 23, 1881, and not only poked fun at the movement, but also included a character that bore a suspicious resemblance to Wilde. Oddly, the writer's popularity only grew. In a stroke of marketing genius, the producer of the play decided to capitalize on Wilde's notoriety and sent him on a tour of North America to present a series of lectures on the English Aesthetic Movement.

When Wilde arrived in Halifax on October 8, 1882, he settled in at the Waverley Inn on Barrington Street before heading to the Academy of Music (now the Maritime Centre) to present his lecture, titled "The Decorative Arts." More than 1,500 Haligonians attended and 400 more showed up the next night for his second lecture, "The House Beautiful."

Despite Wilde's apparent Halifax fan base, some of the city's news editors were less than enthused about his visit. The editors of *The Morning Chronicle* and *The Presbyterian Witness* began a fierce debate about both Oscar Wilde and the Aesthetic Movement. The argument drew plenty of public comment, with one letter to the editor calling Wilde a "narrow-headed, pindled-shanked, shakey [sic], ungraceful specimen of manhood."

36

Three children who died in 1888 are now haunting the Maritime Museum of the Atlantic.

Rumour has it the Maritime Museum of the Atlantic is haunted by three children who died in 1888. When George, Harry, and Ettie May Moxon passed away, they were buried in an unmarked grave, but it was only supposed to be a temporary solution. Their parents, Richard and Elley Moxon, scrimped and saved, and almost thirty years later, they were able to buy a proper headstone for their children.

The headstone was delivered by ship in December 1917 and Richard Moxon asked his friend William Robertson—of Robertson's Hardware & Warehouse—if he would store it for a day or two.

Unfortunately, before Richard had time to retrieve the headstone, the ss *Mont-Blanc* collided with the ss *Imo* in Halifax Harbour, causing an explosion that killed about two thousand people. Richard and Elley died of injuries caused by the Halifax Explosion and, despite efforts made by the Robertson family, no one could find their children's burial site.

With hope that they might someday find the gravesite, the Robertsons continued to store the Moxon children's headstone in their warehouse until 1973, when they closed the business. When the Maritime Museum of the Atlantic took over the space nine years later, they also adopted the headstone.

And, apparently, three small ghosts.

Since then, museum staff members have noticed some strange things. Whether it's a disembodied giggle in an empty hallway, or an arc of water from an unoccupied water fountain, each occurrence has the distinct flavour of a childhood prank.

Although the headstone still resides at the Maritime Museum, the children's grave was found in the Camp Hill Cemetery in 2000, according to descendant Natasha Doreen Moxon.

37

The world's longest-running Gaelic newspaper was first published in Sydney in 1892.

From the road signs to the music, it's obvious that Celtic culture is still alive and well in Cape Breton. And a big part of that proud history is *Mac-Talla*: the all-Gaelic newspaper founded by editor and Inverness resident Jonathan MacKinnon.

MacKinnon, who passed away in 1944, was only twenty-three when he first published the Sydney paper in May 1892. For the first nine years, it was printed weekly, and then bi-weekly, until publication ceased completely in 1904. The paper was a treasure trove of Gaelic song, verse, stories, and articles.

"Mac-Talla" means "echo," and echo it did—all the way across the ocean. During its lifespan, *Mac-Talla* reached more than 1,500 readers across Canada, Scotland, Australia, and New Zealand.

Today, the final volume of *Mac-Talla* has a permanent home in Scotland at the University of the Highlands and Islands, a collection of colleges and research institutions scattered across northern Scotland. Dr. Jacquelyn Thayer Scott presented these valuable cultural documents during a visit to Sabhal Mòr Ostaig, one of the university's colleges, while acting in her former role as president of Cape Breton University. Interestingly, Sabhal Mòr Ostaig is located on the Isle of Skye, where MacKinnon's family originally immigrated from.

38

New France had electricity in 1895—thirty years before the rest of the province.

These days, there's not much more to New France in Digby County than a mark on the map, but from 1895 until 1912, it must have looked pretty futuristic to everyone else living nearby.

In 1892, a man named Jean Jacques Stehelin moved to Digby County from Saint-Charles, France, to exploit Nova Scotia's vast lumber resources. He set up a homestead in the area now known as New France, and dammed Silver River to power his sawmill. Within three years, the rest of his family came over from France and began building up the settlement.

The homestead was expansive: it featured a sawmill, bunkhouse, cookhouse, a huge barn, wine cellar, chapel, clubhouse, and boathouse. It was all powered by electric lights—technology Stehelin had brought over from Europe—and New France became known locally as "Electric City."

The family ran a successful business until 1912, when lumber prices dropped due to the First World War and they were forced to close up shop. The buildings were torn down in the 1950s, and all that remains today are the stone foundations.

39

Nova Scotia's first orchestra played its inaugural concert on April 24, 1897.

Conductor and violinist Max Weil was born in Philadelphia, but landed in Halifax in 1892 after studying violin in Leipzig, Germany, and playing in a New York orchestra. He quickly became an important contributor to the classical music scene in Nova Scotia and spent eight years as head of the violin department at the fledgling Halifax Conservatory of Music. He also founded his own music school (The Weil School of Music) and, most notably, formed the first of two Halifax symphony orchestras.

The orchestra's first concert, which was sponsored by the local council of women, was held at the Academy of Music on Barrington Street. It was a Franz Schubert memorial that included some of the Austrian composer's most famous works, including the "Unfinished Symphony" (Symphony No. 8) and a few works by Weil himself. That first concert featured thirty-six musicians, not including Weil: an eighteen-person string section, eight people on woodwind instruments, eight more on brass, and two in the percussion section.

The orchestra had some significant accomplishments, including a Grand Wagner Concert played in 1900 and accompanied by a massive choir, and a number of concerts played with notable soloists, like legendary pianist Leopold Godowsky. By the time it disbanded in 1908, the orchestra was playing between four and five concerts every season.

40

King George V took a bath in Spa Springs in the 1800s.

Spa Springs, a small Annapolis County community settled by disbanded Loyalist Timothy Ruggles near the end of the American Revolution, has quite a claim to fame. In the eighteenth century, visitors from as far away as Europe visited the spring to enjoy its supposed healing properties. Those visitors included King George V (although at the time, he was just the Prince of Wales), the Earl and Countess of Mulgrave, Samuel Cunard, and Alexander Keith. They each stayed at the Spa Springs Hotel, a resort that featured bathhouses filled with mineral water from the springs.

The belief that the Spa Springs possessed healing properties stems farther back than the eighteenth century—the Mi'kmaq used the water for its regenerative qualities as far back as the 1500s. Another source claims the water is useful for healing cuts, and some modern doctors prescribe very hot mineral baths to counteract the ageing effects of stress and hypertension.

So what's the secret? It might be the gypsum in the groundwater; the water has been filtered through layers of Triassic siltstones, making it incredibly mineral-rich.

41

The winter storm of the twentieth century was Storm King in 1905.

When Nova Scotians talk about major snowstorms, White Juan is almost always the first one mentioned. And that's fair—the fifty to seventy centimetres of snow and driveway avalanches of February 2004 are not easy to forget. But White Juan was no Storm King.

In February 1905, the Maritimes were hit by a devastating snowstorm. Storm King, also known as the "Great Blockage of 1905" and "the winter of the deep snow," dumped up to seven feet of snow on the region; enough of a wallop to bury telephone poles.

The storm caused more damage in 1905 than if it were to hit today, mainly because it totally incapacitated the railroads. Since that was how most communities got their winter supplies of food and coal, it caused major problems. For example, the No. 34 Maritime Express went off the rails in Folly Mountain (previously spelled Folleigh) near Wentworth Valley on February 22 and stayed there, entrenched in snow, until February 26 when it was finally dug out. Men had to shovel snow up embankments thirty feet high to free it.

Unearthing the trapped train was a complicated undertaking. In *A*

The No. 34 Maritime Express train went off the rails and was stuck in snowy Wentworth Valley for four days in 1905. (Nova Scotia Museum)

History of Londonderry, N.S., author Trueman Matheson wrote, "One man stood on the tracks and shoveled [*sic*] the snow as high as he could reach to a ledge above. From there a second worker shoveled the snow to the top of the snowdrift. A third man shoveled the snow off to the side thus it took three men to move one shovelful of snow off the railway tracks."

42

Nova Scotia gold won first prize at the 1907 Jamestown Exposition in Virginia.

In 1907, Lieutenant Governor Duncan Cameron Fraser, Premier George Henry Murray, members of the executive council of Nova Scotia, members of Halifax city council, and hundreds of other Nova Scotians packed up their suitcases and headed to Virginia to show off the province's gold.

In celebration of the three hundredth anniversary of the Jamestown Settlement, the first permanent English settlement in North America, the state of Virginia organized the Jamestown Exposition, which ran from April 26 to December 1, 1907. The exposition was essentially a fair: it boasted exhibits, restaurants, and a number of rides, shows, and attractions that made up an arcade called the "Warpath." All this was scattered between reproductions of various state houses and government buildings. President Roosevelt, Mark Twain, Booker T. Washington, and William Randolph Hurst were among the three million people who attended.

Each day of the exposition celebrated a specific person or theme and, according to a front-page article in *The Miami Metropolis*, October 25, 1907, was deemed "Nova Scotia Day"—possibly in recognition of the fact that Nova Scotia was the only Canadian province with representatives in attendance.

Not only did the group win first prize for its gold exhibit, the article also stated: "Nova Scotia has the most valuable exhibit of gold ore shown at the mines and metallurgy building, and which has resulted in attracting much favorable attention to the Canadian province."

43

Charles Longley opened an amusement park on Deadmans Island in 1907.

In the early 1800s, an internment prison was built on Melville Island (which has since been converted into the Armdale Yacht Club). In its earliest days, the prison's population was mainly British, but that quickly changed during the Napoleonic War and the War of 1812, when French and American prisoners of war filled the tiny, crowded space. Because of the unsanitary conditions and close quarters, diseases like smallpox, scarlet fever, and typhoid ran rampant, claiming many lives. During the nineteenth century, the prison was also used to quarantine patients and to house Black Loyalists. Anyone who died within its walls was buried in an unmarked grave on Deadmans Island. Today, there are about 450 people buried on the little peninsula off Purcells Cove Road.

In 1907, Deadmans Island was sold to Charles Longley, who owned a shipping company called C. F. Longley and Co. He did what is probably one of the most inappropriate things he could have done with the land—he turned it into an amusement park. Melville Park had playground equipment, a dance pavilion, and a ferry system. At one point, three skulls were found on the island and placed in the pavilion to frighten visitors.

In 2005, Deadmans Island Park was established as a memorial for those who are buried there.

Melville Island as it looked in 1888. (Nova Scotia Archives)

44

In the early 1900s, Halifax city hall couldn't hold onto its seized liquor.

On July 10, 1918, Halifax liquor inspector Edward Tracey went to work, expecting to spend a typical day arresting bootleggers. But that morning, the city hall janitor stopped him to say that, according to the masons who were repairing the damage from the Halifax Explosion, Tracey's office door had been found open. Tracey investigated, and discovered that a significant amount of booze was missing from his office: four suitcases containing at least twenty gallons of O. P. rum, and two cases of King George whiskey.

According to a police report, Chief of Police Frank Hanrahan seized two suitcases and twelve tins of rum from a vacant Dartmouth house shortly after Tracey discovered the theft. When two officers and a detective went to the house to investigate further, they found two wooden boxes labelled "King George whiskey," which they showed Tracey. He confirmed that they were the missing boxes and, after interviewing a few more undisclosed sources, Hanrahan charged a man named Clarence Horton with theft.

Interestingly, this was not the first time liquor had gone missing at city hall. According to a *Halifax Herald* article from March 7, 1918, Edward Tracey noticed liquor was missing from his office after the Halifax Explosion. He reported it, and the social service council and the *Halifax Herald* began calling for city council to look into the theft. Accusations began to fly—there were even insinuations that the entire council got into the liquor inspector's stores shortly after the explosion.

A response from Mayor Peter Francis Martin pointed out that since the door to the inspector's office was broken during the explosion, there "was nothing to prevent any one of the hundreds of people who were crowding the passage in front of the office, from helping himself to anything in the room."

45

Two aircraft built in Cape Breton in 1909 were the first to be tested by the Canadian military.

These days, most of us don't even blink when we see a plane flying overhead, but in 1909, a team of four men assembled by Alexander Graham Bell was working hard to make human flight a reality. Casey Baldwin, John McCurdy, Glenn Curtiss, and Thomas Selfridge succeeded on February 23, 1909, when their aerodrome, The Silver Dart, became the first heavier-than-air machine to fly in Canada.

A little over a month later, the four parted ways, but Baldwin and McCurdy continued to work together. The men decided to build two new machines—the Baddeck I and the Baddeck II—which were based on the plans for The Silver Dart, with a couple of improvements. Not only did they replace the silk used in the wings of The Silver Dart with the heavy-duty cloth typically used for boat sails, they also added a slight upward curve to the wing tips.

Within a few months, the director of engineering services for the Canadian Armed Forces heard about the men's work, and invited them to test the aircraft at the Petawawa Military Camp in Ontario. Baldwin and McCurdy selected The Silver Dart and the Baddeck I. On August 2, The

The Silver Dart flying above the frozen Bras d'Or Lake in 1909, something many of those gathered to witness had not believed possible. (Nova Scotia Archives)

Silver Dart was ready to take off, but unfortunately, after three flights, the aerodrome crashed. With The Silver Dart out of commission, the Baddeck I was ready to step into the limelight.

On August 12, 1909, the Baddeck I successfully flew about one hundred feet before experiencing engine trouble. Baldwin and McCurdy tried again the next day, but the aerodrome's propeller and rudder were damaged during a bumpy landing after flying only fifteen feet. Even so, these two Nova Scotia-made aircraft played a significant role in advancing aerodrome technology and making human flight a reality.

46

A luxury car manufacturing company was established in Nova Scotia in 1909.

On October 1, 1908, Ford unveiled the first version of the Model T—a touring vehicle priced at about $1,000. The vehicle was a game changer since the price, which was low compared to other vehicles being manufactured at the time, made owning a car possible for the average citizen. The new car was immediately in high demand, and Ford built a total of 7,728 1908 touring cars.

The same year the Model T was released, Nova Scotia brothers Daniel and John McKay decided to try their hand at automobile manufacturing and rented or purchased (sources vary) Kentville's Nova Scotia Carriage

A 1912 McKay touring car on exhibit at the Nova Scotia Museum of Industry. (Sarah Sawler)

Company facilities—a move that gave them the space they needed to start building cars. The McKay brothers also hired a technical consultant named Archie Pelton, a man who had experience with engines and automobiles. In 1910, Pelton travelled to Detroit, Michigan, and brought back Buda engines and other parts they needed to produce the first Nova Scotia-made car.

The first McKay car was unveiled to the Nova Scotia public in 1910, and although it was priced between $1,450 and $2,300—significantly more expensive than the $850 Model T—it was a luxury vehicle with a frame built by skilled cabinetmakers and blacksmiths.

The company changed its name to the Nova Scotia Carriage and Motor Car Company and moved to Amherst in 1912, but unfortunately that's when things began to fall apart for the McKays. Their new building started sagging at one corner before it was even completed and, with only one hundred cars, they didn't even come close to their production goal of one thousand per year. In 1914, they were forced to close up shop.

47

There was a soda pop factory on McNabs Island until 1915.

For about fifty years, from the mid-1800s until the early 1900s, McNabs Island in Halifax Harbour was happening spot. On a regular basis, the Dartmouth Ferry Service and the Halifax Steamship Service both ferried people to the island to attend large picnics and visit Woolnough's Pleasure Grounds and later, Findlay's Pleasure Grounds. Woolnough's opened in 1873 and featured trails and two pavilions, but when Findlay's opened in 1882, it drew crowds away from Woolnough's with its carnival games and steam-powered merry-go-round.

It didn't take long for McNabs Island to establish its reputation as a high-traffic party spot. In 1846, about six thousand people attended a fundraising picnic for the Mechanics Institute and there are records of over four thousand people visiting the island during the summer of 1880.

So when Halifax meat packer A. J. Davis moved into a big white house on McNabs Island and opened the A. J. Davis Soda Pop Factory, he had easy access to a captive market. A 1991 Nova Scotia Department of Education and Culture document speculates that Davis operated the bottling plant and brewery from 1910 until 1915. During that time, he moistened the lips of island revellers by serving them soda pop and a harder drink, "Pure McNab," in white crocks.

Unfortunately a number of factors, including the Temperance Act and the end of the Sunday ferry service, led to a decline in business on the island and the resulting closure of the factory. Today, all that remains is the stone foundation.

One of the white crocks used to bottle Pure McNab is now part of a vintage bottle collection at the Nova Scotia Museum of Industry. (Sarah Sawler)

48

Arthur Lismer, principal of NSCAD from 1916 to 19, was a member of the Group of Seven.

The Group of Seven, a Canadian collective of self-proclaimed modern landscape artists founded in 1920, challenged the national art scene by rebelling against conservative European aesthetics. They depicted rugged Canadian landscapes in a distinct way—with broad, thickly textured brushstrokes, vibrant colours, and lots of raw emotion. The group was originally comprised of seven men: Franklin Carmichael, A. Y. Jackson, Lawren Harris, Frank Johnston, J. E. H. MacDonald, Frederick Varley, and Arthur Lismer. But just one year before the group was founded, Arthur Lismer was busy running NSCAD University (or The Victoria School, as it was called then) in Halifax.

When Lismer arrived in Halifax in 1916, he had his work cut out for him. According to an essay called "Arthur Lismer: Nova Scotia, 1916–1919," written by curator Gemey Kelly, enrolment at The Victoria School had dropped to about twelve students, and the building was "decrepit." Kelly also excerpted a 1917 letter from Lismer to the director of the National Gallery that blamed the school's directors for the school's poor state:

> The school has been allowed to fall into disuse mainly on account of the lack of interest of its directors who regard art as an exclusive & cultured subject for the edification of the few—& the fewer the students the greater their pride in their connection with it, & its exclusiveness.

Despite his short stint as principal, Lismer made a big impact: by March 1917, he had attracted seventy-two students, and by the end of his tenure, he had established twenty-five scholarships for people of limited means.

49

A seventeen-year-old boy from Dartmouth was a hero during the 1917 Halifax Explosion.

The Halifax Explosion had a number of heroes—some of them better known than others. Horatio Brennan has been recognized for using his tugboat to try and pull the *Mont-Blanc* away from the city before it exploded. Vincent Coleman, the railway dispatcher who sent warning of the impending explosion to Train No. 10 from Saint John, was even honoured with his own Heritage Minute.

But there are many lesser-known heroes, too. One of those is Private Guy Hunter Dillman, a seventeen-year-old resident of Hunter Street in Dartmouth. On the day of the explosion, he risked his life driving a number of sick and injured people to and from the Nova Scotia Hospital in Dartmouth. He didn't escape injury, either—when he finished running his neighbours to the hospital, he collapsed from exhaustion and loss of blood.

There isn't much else known about Private Dillman, except that he was the son of Bertha Dillman, who is recognized as a church mother at Stairs Memorial United Church in Dartmouth. He passed away from influenza on November 23, 1918, while serving in France as a member of the 25th Nova Scotia Battalion.

50

Leon Trotsky was imprisoned in Amherst in 1917.

On March 27, 1917, Russian revolutionary (and eventual foreign minister) Leon Trotsky left New York with his wife, two children, and a few other Russians on the SS *Kristianiafjord* to return to their homeland. It was just twelve days after Russian ruler Czar Nicholas II was forced to abdicate his throne and, according to a passage in *My Life* by Trotsky, they were "sent off in a deluge of flowers and speeches, for [they] were going to the country of the revolution."

But when they stopped in Halifax, things weren't so rosy. While the steamship was being checked over, Canadian officials interrogated the Russian passengers about their political convictions. According to Trotsky's autobiography, two detectives named Machen and Westwood were convinced that Trotsky and his entourage were dangerous and had the group hauled off the boat.

Trotsky's wife and kids remained in the Port of Halifax, but he and the other Russians were taken to the Amherst Internment Camp—the former Canadian Car & Foundry. The only explanation for the sudden removal

Amherst Internment Camp was the largest prisoner-of-war (POW) camp in Canada during the First World War. (Nova Scotia Archives)

offered by camp commander Colonel Morris was, "You are dangerous to the present Russian government."

Trotsky settled in with the eight hundred other men living in what he described as "an old and very dilapidated iron foundry that had been confiscated from its German owner," and he quickly made friends and gained supporters.

Three weeks later, on April 20, 1917, the British Admiralty agreed to release him when, according to Trotsky, "the Soviets stepped in." Trotsky and his family set sail for Russia soon after and, just like when he left New York, he received a spectacular send-off: "Although the officers shut themselves up in their compartment, and only a few poked their noses through the chinks, the sailors and workers lined the passage on both sides, an improvised band played the revolutionary march, and friendly hands were extended to us from every quarter."

51

A mob of people drove a police car into Halifax Harbour in May 1918.

Plug the keywords "Halifax" and "riot" into a Google search, and you'll get a long list of results with information on the VE Day Riots. Although May 7 and 8, 1945, were very significant days in Halifax's history—resulting in 211 people being arrested and 564 businesses being damaged—it certainly wasn't the first time Haligonians went on a rampage.

On May 25, 1918, a drunken crewmember of the HMCS *Niobe* wandered into a popular Barrington Street shop called the 5 & 10 Cent Store. It was a Saturday night, and the store was packed. When the sailor tried to steal an item from the store, the storeowner called the police. Two officers arrived and simply removed the sailor from the store, but when he was sent outside, he ambled down Barrington Street, using "the filthiest kind of language," according to a report later written by the chief of police. His bad behaviour got him arrested and, as the police were bringing him to the station, some soldiers who were trying to "rescue" the sailor stopped them. The soldiers were also arrested.

Later that night, an angry mob made up of soldiers, sailors, and a few civilians gathered outside of Halifax's city hall to protest the arrests. When the police refused to release the prisoners, the crowd rioted. They broke windows, attempted to light city hall on fire, injured firemen and policemen, and drove a police motorcycle and a patrol car into Halifax Harbour. According to a May 27, 1918, *Halifax Herald* article, a man was heard shouting, "Let's dump the blooming thing in the harbour!" as he and a couple of other men drove the patrol car down George Street, towards the Market Wharf (now the Cable Wharf).

According to a letter from Halifax Police Chief Frank Hanrahan to the chief commissioner of police in Ottawa dated June 12, 1918, the Halifax police lacked the manpower to manage the crisis, and asked the military for assistance. Unfortunately, Hanrahan wasn't able to reach a superior officer, so he called the Citadel, and was referred to a Colonel Thompson. The letter goes on to say, "About ten o'clock, a small detachment of infantry arrived. They were of little service, as in some instances, the rioters took the bayonets out of the rifles of the soldiery."

Eventually, the navy saved poor Hanrahan. The sailor who started the whole mess was handed over to his ship's master-at-arms, and the rioting soldiers were left in military custody. When the case went to trial, the sailor pleaded guilty. The rioters went to trial as well, but they were still waiting to go to a "superior court" when Hanrahan's letter was penned.

暴徒洗劫了哈利法克斯的中国餐馆.

52

Rioters ransacked Halifax's Chinese restaurants in 1919.

引入
中国
人头税
The late 1800s and early 1900s were challenging times for Chinese Canadians. Not only did racism abound across Canada, the country also introduced the Chinese Head Tax: a fee charged to every Chinese immigrant who came to Canada. When the tax was introduced in 1885, it was $50, but as more and more people were able to afford it, the tax increased exponentially. By 1903, it had risen to $500—almost two years' salary for the average Chinese immigrant.

In 1923, things got even worse with the introduction of the Chinese Immigration Act. Not only did Chinese immigration become extremely limited—only fifty Chinese people immigrated to Canada during the twenty-four years the act was in effect—but the act also restricted immigrants from bringing their families with them.

In the early 1900s a rash of race riots occurred across the country, and on the evening of February 18, 1919, one erupted in Halifax. For over two hours, several hundred rioters attacked and looted six popular Chinese restaurants on Gottingen, Brunswick, and Barrington Streets. The rioters caused thousands of dollars' worth of damage to The Crown Café, Busy Bee, Nova Scotia Café, Allie's Café, Victory Café, and the Frisco Café.

According to a *Halifax Herald* article printed on February 20, 1919, the riot raged out of control again the next night, but there was "no rhyme nor reason" for the "night's display of brute force." The newspaper also cast blame on a number of people: returned soldiers, bootleggers, hooligans, vandals, and German spies.

根据 1919年 2月20日 出版的《哈法先驱报》

第二天晚上暴乱 再次失控

53

St. Philip's African Orthodox Church in Whitney Pier began as a toolshed in 1928.

At 34 Hankard Street in Whitney Pier, Cape Breton, you'll find a small white church with a fascinating history—and much of it is deeply rooted in the Sydney steel industry.

In 1899 Dominion Coal owner Henry Melville Whitney decided to branch out into steel, with a little help from the local and federal governments. This bit of inspiration resulted in the birth of Dominion Iron and Steel Company Limited (DISCO).

Around the time DISCO was established, Whitney started recruiting African American workers. And about fifteen years after that, he sent two steelworkers to Barbados to recruit more. The Black community in Sydney Mines began to grow quickly, and these individuals started looking for a church.

Unfortunately, there was a significant amount of racial tension, and although there were—and still are—many churches in Whitney Pier, members of the Black community weren't allowed through their doors.

In 1921, Whitney Pier's Black community formed their own congregation by joining the African Orthodox Church, a denomination founded earlier that year, and started meeting regularly. They had to move their meeting space twice before settling permanently on Hankard Street in 1928.

When they purchased the Hankard Street land, DISCO gave or leased (sources vary) the congregation of the African Orthodox Church an old toolshed to renovate. They took apart the toolshed and dragged the pieces by horse to the church's current location, where the materials were repurposed to form the St. Philip's African Orthodox Church.

54

Nova Scotians drove on the left-hand side of the road until 1923.

At 2:00 A.M. on April 15, 1923, the rules of the road changed for Nova Scotian motorists. The Honourable William Chisholm proposed the bill, which passed in March, because New Brunswick had already switched to right-side driving, and those who crossed the border between provinces were having trouble adjusting.

The fact that the transition went smoothly was somewhat miraculous. Although newspapers throughout Nova Scotia published plenty of public notices, it seems the provincial government dropped the ball—at least according to an article published by the *Amherst Daily News* berating them for failing to run a publicity campaign in advance of the change. The government did eventually issue large windshield stickers reminding oncoming traffic to "Keep to the right," which took up approximately a quarter of the windshield.

The switch also had financial ramifications for some within the province—namely, the owners of the electric railway system and Lunenburg's beef farmers. Nova Scotia Tramways & Power Company Limited sued the province for the costs required to move the doors from the left side of their trams to the right, while people who were unable to retrain their oxen to walk on the right-hand side of the road were forced to slaughter them, ultimately driving down the cost of beef in the province.

55

Lake William's annual Guides Meets attracted thousands between 1929 and 1943.

B eginning in 1929, wilderness guides from all over Canada gathered at Lake William in Lunenburg County for their annual Guides Meet, an event that offered a vast array of competitions, including canoe racing, log rolling, kettle boiling, and log chopping. But there was much more to the Guides Meets than just competitions; there was also plenty of showmanship. The acts differed from year to year, but some of the performers included sharpshooters, clowns, unicyclists, jugglers, magicians, singers, and even a contortionist named Tiny Divine.

The week-long event was held on a piece of property spanning about one hundred acres that was turned into a campground for the event. At the Meet's peak popularity, those grounds held over 1,300 tents, and the daily attendance ranged from ten to twelve thousand people.

Admission was twenty-five cents per day, and you could get breakfast for thirty-five cents, lunch for fifty cents, and supper for forty cents.

The Guides Meets were held each year until 1943. By that time, many of the guides had gone to war, and a gas shortage made it difficult for those who remained to travel to Lake William.

56

The 1930 murder of Pictou resident John William Dryden was never solved.

On May 5, 1930, Albert Holden and John Graham visited the home of their seventy-three-year-old neighbour, John William Dryden. They were worried; they hadn't seen the sawmill worker for several days.

When they arrived, they found a gruesome sight: Dryden was dead in his bed with a massive head wound. It was clear that someone had attacked him with a sharp, heavy object while he was sleeping and left him lying there, blood soaking onto the pillow beneath his head. Dryden didn't have much of value, but his watch was missing, and his bankbook had been tossed on the floor.

Dryden's body was examined by a coroner in Stellarton, who gave the opinion that he'd been killed with an axe and that the blow had fractured his right mastoid bone, causing him to hemorrhage and die instantly. Sources report different murder weapons—a sensational article in the *Truro Daily News*, published on May 7, 1930, states, "A monkey wrench, 18 inches long, three and a half inches wide at the jaws and one and a half inch thick is believed to have been the death-dealing weapon used by the murderer of John W. Dryden in one of the most brutal murders ever perpetrated in Pictou County."

Three suspects were arrested and tried in the murder: a Sherbrooke man named James Stewart, a Musquodoboit man named Arthur Fisher, and a Irishman named William J. McDonald who had arrived in Nova Scotia less than a year earlier and regularly carried a suspiciously large amount of cash.

There was plenty of finger-pointing throughout the trials, with McDonald claiming to have seen Stewart kill Dryden with an axe and Stewart and Fisher denying everything. In the end, there was not enough evidence to convict Stewart or Fisher and they were released. McDonald, however, was charged with contempt of court—in earlier trials he got into loud arguments with the prosecution, and in later trials he simply refused to speak.

Dryden's body was buried on May 9 in the Lorne Street Cemetery under a headstone that reads, "Murdered 1930."

57

Scotiabank's head office was built in 1931 and the design features lots of Nova Scotia wildlife.

John M. Lyle was an architect who studied in Paris, worked in New York City, and then moved on to Toronto in 1906, where he made his mark by designing the Royal Alexandra Theatre and Union Station. But one of his most notable accomplishments was in Halifax: Scotiabank's Atlantic regional office on the corner of Hollis and Prince Streets. He was commissioned to design the building in 1930 and just one year later, the new building opened its doors, revealing ornate architecture that celebrates Nova Scotia's natural diversity.

When Lyle accepted the commission, he was determined to create something that accurately reflected the unique natural aspects of Nova Scotia. He began intensively researching Maritime plants, animals, and marine life. The enormous banking room has an impressively detailed ceiling decorated with octagonal panels featuring beavers, rabbits, turkeys, foxes, and fish. The bronze and monel doors that block off the staircase leading to the Safety Deposit Department incorporate squirrels, birds, and beavers.

The stonework on the outside of the building is just as significant: alongside carvings representing the Sydney Steel Plant and a sailing ship, there are bears, geese, and seahorses. Even the window grilles form the bodies of codfish.

The building is now considered historically significant by Halifax's heritage property program.

58

The world's oldest known hockey stick was made in Cape Breton in the 1930s.

In early 2015, the Canadian Museum of History in Gatineau, Quebec, tapped into the National Collection Fund to purchase the oldest known hockey stick—the "Moffatt Stick"—from Nova Scotia resident Mark Presley for $300,000.

The stick originally belonged to Cape Bretoner William "Dilly" Moffatt, who was born in 1929. It's a short-handled stick, made from a single piece of sugar maple harvested in the 1930s, and it features Dilly's initials carved into the blade.

The Moffatt family held onto the artifact until the 1980s, when they gave it to a local barbershop. It sat on display there for almost thirty years before Mark Presley happened upon it and bought it for $1,000.

After making the purchase, Presley started digging around. He spoke to Charlie Moffatt, Dilly's grandson, who told him that Dilly used to play hockey on Pottle Lake in North Sydney. Presley, sensing he may have stumbled upon a priceless piece of Canadian history, requested the stick be examined at Mount Allison University in New Brunswick to determine its age.

The Moffatt Stick will be displayed in the Canadian History Hall at the national museum—just in time for Canada's 150th anniversary.

59

Hal Foster, creator of the popular 1930s comic strip *Prince Valiant*, was born in Halifax.

In 1921, Hal Foster left Winnipeg to go on a 1,600-kilometre bike ride that he hoped would lead him to a stable job and a chance to study at the Chicago Art Institute. The journey took fourteen days but it was worth it—Foster's journey to Chicago marked the beginning of his remarkable career in comics.

When Foster arrived, he enrolled in night classes at the Chicago Art Institute, the National Academy of Design, and the Chicago Academy of Fine Arts. He worked in the magazine industry for a while, but everything changed in 1929, when he was asked to illustrate the comic strip adaptation of *Tarzan*. The adventure strip was wildly successful, but by the mid-1930s Foster was working on an adventure strip called *Prince Arn*. The project was later renamed *Prince Valiant,* and it was so popular that the Duke of Windsor himself called it "the greatest contribution to English literature in the past hundred years."

Years before all of this, Foster lived in Halifax. In fact, he lived the first thirteen years of his life there, in a home on the corner of Lower Water and Fawson Streets built by his great-grandfather, Francis Stevens. Foster loved the sea, and demonstrated an adventurous spirit early on, when he took a raft across Halifax Harbour at age eight.

It's possible Foster's early experiences inspired the work that would eventually influence some of history's

King Arthur knights Prince Valiant, circa 1941–42. (Copyright Hal Foster, courtesy of Fantagraphics Books)

greatest comic artists—Jack Kirby (*Ant-Man, Iron Man, Avengers*), Charles Vess (*The Amazing Spiderman, Neil Gaiman and Charles Vess' Stardust, Swamp Thing*), and Mark Schultz (*Xenozoic Tales, Conan, The Flash*).

60

Central Grove in Digby County published Canada's tiniest newspaper between 1933 and 1943.

Every Thursday for ten years—from 1933 to 1943—the people of Central Grove would trade in their quarters for the latest issue of *The Tiny Tattler*, a newspaper run by locals Ivan Shortcliffe and Rupert Cann. The paper claimed to be "Canada's Smallest Newspaper," and was recognized as such by the federal government at the time.

The weekly publication was small but mighty. Its readership grew from eighteen to about five thousand over the ten-year span, and copies were sent as far away as Europe and South Africa. *The Tiny Tattler* certainly didn't shy away from much—according to a website dedicated to the history of the paper, Shortcliffe and Cann once received death threats when they published a story that exposed a rum-running operation.

But the average *Tattler* article wasn't nearly so serious; the paper delighted in the everyday goings-on in Central Grove. Some headlines from back issues include the following:

- Mrs. Sheldon Morrell, of Westport, spent Sunday with her father, Mr. Geo. Delaney.
- Mrs. Jesse Powell, of Tiverton, is visiting her daughter, Mrs. J. S. Pyrne.
- Miss Pauline Delaney is staying at the residence of Lloyd Blackford.
- Mr. Edw Blackford of Tiverton, W. Gidney of Mink Cove and F. Height of North Range were in town recently.
- As a souvenir of the first deer he shot, Byron Delaney of Central Grove had the horns sent to the US and had them fitted for handles on a silver knife and fork.

61

The Hindenburg almost collided with Cape Breton's Grand Narrows Bridge in 1937.

Most of us know the story of the Hindenburg: the massive, 430,950-pound, 245-metre-long German airship that killed twenty-two crew-members and thirteen passengers when it caught fire as it attempted to land near Lakeport, New Jersey, on May 6, 1937. According to an accident investigation report published by the United States Department of Commerce on August 15, 1937, the disaster was the result of a hydrogen leak.

The accident report says the journey across the Atlantic had been "uneventful," with the exception of some fairly typical turbulence. But if Cape Breton spectators are to be believed, the Hindenburg had a close call while flying over the island on May 5, 1937. Residents reported seeing the airship pass overhead and just miss the Grand Narrows Bridge.

"Big Gordie" MacNeil, a veteran of the First World War, had quite the stockpile of artillery in his barn, according to the *Cape Breton Book of Days*. When he saw the airship flying over "his territory," he headed to the barn to find a Lewis gun and some ammunition. His colonel, William G. MacRae, who happened to be with him at the time, stopped him from taking the shot, effectively preventing an explosion that would have been triggered if the tracers in MacNeil's bullets met the hydrogen in the Hindenburg.

It is possible that Cape Bretoners were simply tired of ducking whenever the Hindenburg went by. The September 29, 1936, issue of the *Montreal Gazette* noted that when the Hindenburg passed over the Bras d'Or Lakes earlier that day, it came within twenty feet of the water before regaining altitude.

62

Babe Ruth used to take regular hunting and fishing trips to Nova Scotia in the 1930s.

Revered baseball pitcher and outfielder George Herman "Babe" Ruth is known for his 714 home runs and his impressive .342 batting average, but there was more to him than baseball. He also spent plenty of time hunting and fishing along North America's east coast—from Nova Scotia to Florida—and he tracked everything from alligators and wild turkeys to moose and black bears.

Although he hunted and fished in Nova Scotia a number of times, Babe Ruth's 1935 visit to Yarmouth was particularly well documented.

L to R: Bob Edge, local guide; Babe Ruth; "Deadeye" Jack Matthews, friend of Ruth's.
Somewhere on Water Street in Yarmouth, circa 1935.
(Yarmouth County Museum Archives)

SARAH SAWLER

According to an *Outdoor Life* article from 1937 titled "Babe's in the Woods," the baseball legend visited the small town in the fall of 1935 and was followed around by crowds of people until he settled at a hunting camp owned by William Lovitt. He began his visit with some target practice and, according to Bob Edge, the journalist who wrote the article, Ruth was a "snap shooter, as quick as lightning, and he can drill a tomato can at sixty yards."

The hunting portion of the trip began at 4:00 A.M. the next day. With a canoe and some chewing tobacco, Ruth and his party took off for the woods, where he shot his first buck within twenty-four hours, frightened off a female moose and its calf by brandishing a tree root, wrestled an ox, and took down a bear.

63

The first systematic recordings of Gaelic songs took place in Cape Breton in 1937.

Although the Gaelic language's deepest roots are in Scotland, Gaelic songs were first recorded for study in Cape Breton.

In 1937, Scottish historian John Lorne Campbell visited the island with his wife. He had been to Cape Breton a few years before and, after a few years in Barra, he decided to return, this time with a wax cylinder recorder. Campbell studied Scottish Gaelic and was a member of the Gaelic Club at Oxford, so it's not surprising that he had a special interest in recording Gaelic folk songs when he returned. These Gaelic recordings are now found at Campbell's Canna House in Scotland. Notably, he was also the first person to record the spoken Mi'kmaw language.

Over the next couple of decades, folklorist Helen Creighton and academic Charles William Dunn, who would eventually become chair of Harvard University's Department of Celtic Languages and Literature, also collected an impressive number of Gaelic folk song recordings.

In Scotland, however, no one systematically recorded Gaelic folk songs until 1946, when the Irish Folklore Commission sent Calum Iain Maclean to the island of Raasay. According to Maclean's diary, he had been raised on the island and had seen many folk tales and songs die with the people who told them. In an effort to preserve what was left, he collected an enormous amount of material, including the longest story ever recorded in Scotland.

64

Chéticamp resident Marguerite Gallant started a vast collection of the region's artifacts in 1938.

Marguerite Gallant of Chéticamp was a remarkable woman. At age eleven, she began working as a maid for people who needed a little extra help—some were ill, others were elderly. During her teenage years, she moved to Pennsylvania and began working for a Mrs. Cahill, whose husband, Edward, was an amateur collector.

In 1938, when Marguerite was in her late forties, the Gallants moved back into a small house in Chéticamp and brought along an enormous six-leaf table that the Cahill family gave Marguerite as a parting gift. The table was just the start: according to Les Trois Pignons Cultural Centre, Gallant had caught the collecting bug from Edward Cahill, and from 1938 until she

Marguerite Gallant shows off some of her collectables at Les Trois Pignons Cultural Centre in Chéticamp, circa 1980. (From La Société Saint-Pierre collection)

passed away in 1983, Gallant collected anything and everything—shells, rocks, photographs, dolls, and any other objects her neighbours brought over when they couldn't find room in their own homes.

Visitors were always welcome. According to an account by Beatrice Gallant, a relative of Marguerite's and curator of Les Trois Pignons Cultural Centre, so many people visited Marguerite that she started keeping a guest book. Often, those visitors would spend time around the ten-foot table that spanned Marguerite's entire kitchen.

Today, that table is part of a valuable collection of Chéticamp artifacts preserved at Le Centre de Trois Pignons, a cultural centre and museum in Inverness County, Cape Breton. The rest of Marguerite's collection resides there, alongside a separate collection of stunning hooked rugs by Elizabeth LeFort and a variety of other household artifacts collected by the centre.

65

Bedford's famous Chickenburger was actually a chicken roll until the 1940s.

In 1939, Salter Innes convinced his son and daughter-in-law—Jack and Bernice Innes—to buy a piece of property across the street from Bedford's Sunnyside Restaurant. At the time, the property, known locally as "The Shadyside" (get it?), featured a number of small attractions, including a mini-golf course, a dance hall, and a canteen. The Chickenburger, as it exists today, grew out of that canteen.

Because the three entrepreneurs wanted to expand beyond the usual fried fare, they decided to sell chicken rolls, which—after some experimentation—were comprised of chopped chicken in a steamed hot dog bun. They were five cents each.

Since the Second World War was in full swing, rationing was a key concern. Canada (and many other countries) implemented price controls in order to prevent radical inflation during a time of scarce resources. This posed a problem for the Innes family since, according to a book self-published by the Chickenburger in 2010, "in order to turn a healthy profit, they'd need to charge more for the sandwich."

Ever the sharp businessman, Salter realized that the price controls only applied to existing products, so if he changed the bun, he could change the price. He did both, leaving Bedford with the chicken burgers they enjoy today.

66

Many of Chéticamp's earliest folk songs are preserved in songbooks published between 1942 and 1993.

Chéticamp's earliest folk songs, which often had accompanying dances, were imported from France and Quebec. Although people often sang them by memory and without instrumental accompaniment, these early songs were repeated often enough that they survived multiple generations.

Today, thanks to Père Anselme Chiasson and Père Daniel Boudreau, Acadians don't have to rely solely on memory to access their ancestral folk music. In 1942, the two men produced the first volume in a series of songbooks called *Chansons d'Acadie*. It's an extensive collection—eleven volumes were published between 1942 and 1993—and it's a varied one, too. The first edition contains the Acadian national anthem and a song called "La Passion," whose origins date back to the twelfth century. The collection also contains songs from the Chéticamp parish in Cape Breton.

Acadian choirs draw heavily on this collection, and it likely had a hand in inspiring modern Chéticamp musicians, who have begun to produce and record their own original songs. Marc Boudreau, who's been fiddling since he was nine, and songstress Chrissy Crowley are just a couple of the popular musicians who have emerged from the area.

67

Dwayne "The Rock" Johnson's father was born in Nova Scotia in 1944.

Lots of people recognize the man behind wrestling moves "The People's Elbow" and "The Rock Bottom," but not many know where he came from. Although the wrestler-turned-actor was born in California, his mother, Ata Maivia, is from Hawaii, and his father, Wayde Douglas Bowles (better known as Rocky Johnson), is from Nova Scotia.

Born in Amherst in 1944, Bowles is a descendent of James Bowles, a Black Loyalist who emigrated from New York to Annapolis Royal after the American Revolution.

Bowles left Amherst for Toronto when he was just sixteen and started training as a boxer. Although he studied boxing—he even sparred with greats like Muhammad Ali and George Foreman—The Rock's father had always been drawn to wrestling and eventually switched his focus. As a boy, he attended wrestling matches in Amherst, and in 1969, he returned to the Amherst Stadium to defend his Canadian heavyweight championship.

For almost thirty years, Bowles wrestled as the Soulman and Sweet Ebony Diamond, and took home prominent titles like the 1967 Canadian tag title (with Don Leo Jonathan), the 1969 North America Champion title (1969), and the 1983–84 World Wrestling Federation tag championship (with Tony Atlas).

After his retirement in 1991, Bowles became a wrestling trainer for World Wrestling Entertainment (WWE). His clients included Brock Lesnar, Sylvain Grenier, and—you guessed it—his son, Dwayne "The Rock" Johnson.

68

The City of Halifax used Africville as a dumping ground from 1858 to 1967.

Drive along the Bedford Highway towards the North End of Halifax, pass a container pier, and make a left turn onto Africville Road. Drive just a couple more minutes, and you'll see a small yellow church. That's the Africville Museum, a replica of the original church that was bulldozed by the City of Halifax, in the middle of the night, in 1967. The replica was built as a part of the city's 2010 apology for "historic wrongs"— wrongs that include forcing an entire community to relocate with extremely little compensation.

The community of Africville has land deeds stretching back to 1848, when Black settlers bought land in the area. Many people believe that Africville was solely a Black community, but its population was multicultural.

Although the City of Halifax framed Africville as a slum, its residents paid taxes like everyone else—and received very little in return. They had

Since they did not receive water and sewer service like the rest of Halifax, Africville residents relied on community wells, circa 1965. (Nova Scotia Archives)

no running water, sewers, health or police services, or electricity despite multiple requests.

In 1858, the city closed its sewage disposal pits and moved them to Africville. The area was also used as a dumping ground for any other "undesirable services" the city wanted out of the downtown. These included the large, open city dump (labelled a health risk by city council and placed just one hundred metres from residents' homes in 1955), the Rockhead Prison, at least one slaughterhouse, a fertilizer plant, and the Infectious Diseases Hospital.

69

A third of Halifax city council tried to block CBC from setting up on Bell Road in 1954.

After more than fifty years, CBC's Bell Road location was just part of the landscape for most Haligonians—until the corporation's move to Chebucto Road in 2014—but in 1954, selling the land was a hot button issue. CBC had offered to purchase the land for $45,000 and in January 1954, the proposal was brought before city council.

Aldermen Ahern, DeWolf, Adams, and Kitz all voted against the sale. DeWolf argued against it because an unnamed "very distinguished citizen of Halifax" wasn't happy about it. Kitz thought it was a poor business decision and, based on the minutes, Adams didn't say anything of note at all. Ahern made an alternative suggestion: "Why not shove them over to that portion of the City Field that is run down?"

In the end, the majority of council agreed to sell, perhaps because of Alderman Lane's convincing argument that the general population of Halifax wanted to make use of their new TVs. "You know how many television sets are being bought in this city with nothing coming in?" he asked. "To vote against this is to obstruct a little bit of progress in this community."

A little more than two years later, CBC's CBHT-TV opened their new building on Bell Road and began producing shows like *Mrs. Byng's Boarders*, *The Alibi Room*, and *The Don Messer Show*. Finally, the people of Halifax had something to watch on their static-filled TVs.

70

From 1963 to 1968, Halifax's Grace Maternity Hospital ran a contraception clinic.

The 1960s were tumultuous years for the women's reproductive rights movement. The criminal code of the time made selling and advertising contraceptives illegal (the punishment was two years in jail). Condoms could be found, but they weren't reliable because their production was not regulated.

There was a loophole in the criminal code that allowed doctors to provide women with IUDs, diaphragms, or the pill as long as it was done "in the public good," but most family doctors weren't willing to toe the line. Those who were willing generally only provided these services to married women.

But for five years, beginning in 1963, the Grace Maternity Hospital in Halifax offered a solution to women who wanted to control their own fertility. As a teaching hospital (public good, anyone?), it was able to legally provide spermicides, condoms, diaphragm fittings, and information on how to properly use the rhythm method.

Unfortunately, the clinic was poorly attended for a number of reasons: it was difficult to access because of its location, a lack of advertising, and a huge social stigma. The clinic closed after only five years—despite the obvious need for its services.

The clinic was ahead of its time—in 1969, things began to change (albeit slowly) when Prime Minister Pierre Trudeau legalized the sale and advertisement of contraception.

71

In the 1960s, The Black Panther Party helped influence social change in Nova Scotia.

In 1968, Halifax civil rights activist Burnley Allan "Rocky" Jones attended the four-day Montreal Congress of Black Writers. While he was there, he met Stokely Carmichael, a Trinidadian American civil rights activist and "Honorary Prime Minister" of the Black Panther Party. The two men hit it off, and Jones invited Carmichael and his wife, folk singer and activist Miriam Makeba ("Mama Africa"), to come back with him to Halifax for a visit.

When Carmichael and Jones arrived in the city, there was an uproar. Police were everywhere, and there was serious racial tension. But the visit started something great; just one month later, there was a historic meeting—one that attracted over four hundred Black Nova Scotians from all across the province, as well as a couple of Black Panthers. The topic of the meeting, which was held on November 30, 1968, was the racial inequality that plagued the province, and the necessity of an organization to advocate for Black Nova Scotians.

Despite the initial uproar, the meeting not only ended peacefully, it inspired the creation of something very important—the Black United Front of Nova Scotia. For the next twenty-seven years, the organization was instrumental in creating social change within Nova Scotia—it helped people find work, access government programs, obtain legal assistance, and offered mediation and counselling to schools.

72

In 1967, a Cape Breton steelworker became the first Black Canadian appointed to the Order of Canada.

If you check out the website for the Governor General of Canada and dig around a bit, you'll find a listing for Isaac C. Phills, appointed to the Order of Canada on July 6, 1967. Under a table providing his name, honour received, location, appointment date, and investiture date, is a short description:

> A Cape Breton steel worker of West Indian origin, who raised a large family and despite many difficulties, gave them a good education and start in life and set a fine example in the community. Deceased on March 9, 1985.

It's an accurate description, but he deserves more. In 1916, Phills, who was a horticulturalist, moved from Barbados to Whitney Pier with his wife, Ada. He was hoping to procure land to farm, but shortly after he arrived, he realized he could not get the land he needed, and there were no farming jobs available. So, after a stint in the Armed Forces, he took a job at the Sydney Steel Plant—where he worked for forty-five years—and raised seven children with his wife.

It was a tough time to live in Sydney—the family lived through the Great Depression—but despite rampant illness and the challenges presented by workers' strikes and a plant layoff in 1946, Phills managed to provide his children with the education they needed to pursue jobs in medicine, science, and education.

Isaac Phills, photo by Abbass Studios Ltd., in 1960. (Beaton Institute, Cape Breton University, A-6419.1)

73

Haligonian Owen McCarron created the Marvel Fun and Games series, which ran throughout the 1970s and '80s.

For years, Haligonian Owen McCarron was an advertising director at the *Chronicle-Herald* in Halifax. During his time there, he created *Owen McCarron's Fun and Games*, a regular fixture in both the *Herald* and the *Mail Star*.

McCarron was also an extremely successful independent publisher. He owned both McCarron Advertising and Comic Book World, and freelanced with DC Comics, Marvel Comics, and Charlton Comics (which closed in 1985 after selling most of its character rights to DC). His body of work is impressive and includes the original Ghost Rider series, *Spidey Super Stories,* and *Marvel Fun and Games*, a popular puzzle book that was the result of McCarron's successful pitch to Stan Lee himself.

McCarron loved history, and believed that comic books can be used to educate as well as entertain. His characters Sammy Seagull and Captain Enviro demonstrate this philosophy and McCarron was awarded a Nova Scotia Environment Award for "advancing green concerns." He also created many historical comics over his thirty-two years with the *Chronicle-Herald*, including an annual page dedicated to examining different aspects of the Halifax Explosion.

In 2006, one year after his death at age seventy-six, McCarron was inducted into the Canadian Comic Book Hall of Fame, an illustrious roster that also includes Joe Shuster, co-creator of *Superman*; Todd McFarlane, creator of *Spawn*; and Richard Comely, co-creator of *Captain Canuck*.

74

In 1974, The Nova Scotia Association of Architects made up a holiday called National Beaver Day, and they celebrated it every year until 2015.

February 28, 1974 was a landmark day for Canadian beavers; it was the first day the rodent enjoyed a holiday in its honour. In response to CBC radio host Peter Gzowski's call for a new national holiday, the Nova Scotia Association of Architects (NSAA) proposed Beaver Day. For the architects, it just made sense to recognize the beaver: apart from the stereotypical Canadian symbolism, beavers hold a special resonance for architects—they're natural builders, after all.

In the late 1980s, a Halifax architect named Ted Brown wrote to parliament asking them to consider officially making Beaver Day a national holiday, to no avail. But that didn't stop the NSAA from celebrating it. Each year, on the final Friday of February, the NSAA held an annual luncheon where they presented two awards: The Order of the Beaver Award, given to those who made valuable contributions to the field of architecture, to Canada as a whole, or to beavers as a species; and the Beaver Droppings Award, which was often awarded to a celebrity or politician for less than valuable contributions to the above categories.

Beaver Day was celebrated each year from 1974 up until 2015, when Nova Scotia announced a new February holiday (Nova Scotia Heritage Day). Since a February holiday was the ultimate goal of the enterprise, Beaver Day is no longer officially celebrated by the NSAA.

75

In 1983, Nova Scotian Dr. Marie Hamilton was the first Black Canadian woman to receive the Governor General's Award.

After a lifetime of hard work and dedication to her community, Dr. Marie Hamilton was awarded the 1983 Governor General's Award in Commemoration of the Persons Case.

The award is inspired by the efforts of five women who, in the late 1920s, fought for women's right to hold seats in the senate. The group of women from Alberta, dubbed "The Famous Five," included Nellie McClung, Henrietta Muir Edwards, Irene Parlby, Louise McKinney, and Emily Murphy. In 1929 their efforts paid off and Canada's highest court of appeal ruled that the word "person" included both men and women, allowing both sexes to hold office in the senate.

"The Persons Case," as it's now known, was the inspiration for the Governor General's Award in Commemoration of the Persons Case, which was created in 1979 to commemorate the case's fiftieth anniversary. Since then, this annual award has been presented to five women who demonstrate the same strength, courage, and effort as the Famous Five.

Dr. Hamilton's efforts, which included tireless work with the Halifax North End Volunteers for Seniors, the Congress of Black Women of Nova Scotia, and the Women's Institute of the African United Baptist Association, continues to be recognized today by Halifax Public Libraries and their annual Dr. Marie Hamilton Award, which is presented to an exemplary junior high school student.

76

Halifax's Mardi Gras celebrations drew more than 40,000 people in the 1980s and '90s.

B etween the 1980s and '90s, Halifax developed a Canada-wide reputation for its annual Mardi Gras celebration. The event drew more than forty thousand revellers every Halloween, most of them dressed in elaborate costumes. And, according to a 2005 article in *The Coast* called "Trick or Street" by Lezlie Lowe, many of those forty thousand people were likely hiding lemon gin in their pants.

The evening began as something of a family affair but as the night wore on and families went home, partygoers packed the streets. They wore everything from Freddy Krueger and Frankenstein costumes to giant, handcrafted beer bottles. Streets were closed down to accommodate the celebration and the night was filled with shouts, laughter, and the occasional buzz of Freddy's chainsaw.

But after a few years, people became concerned about the public cost of this event—the cleanup alone was nothing to sneeze at. There were growing problems with public drinking, sexual assaults, and violence. In a 1990 council meeting, Alderman Fitzgerald pointed out that the night was nothing more than "a drunken brawl." As a result, alcohol was banned on the streets in 1990, and over time, the event began to wane.

Over the next few years, a few local businesspeople tried to revitalize it—Dale Thompson, who founded the Halifax International Busker Festival, even suggested that it stretch over three days. But all attempts failed and by 1995, the event had fizzled.

77

Road rage caused by the Micmac Rotary in Dartmouth inspired a 1982 song.

The Province of Nova Scotia built the notorious Micmac Rotary in Dartmouth during the early 1960s. It stayed, causing rush hour road rage, until the 1990s when the Micmac Parclo (named for its partial cloverleaf shape) replaced it. While it existed, the Micmac Rotary connected Highway 111 with Route 318 (Braemar Drive/Waverley Road) and Trunk 7 (Main Street/Prince Albert Road/Graham's Grove).

Many drivers remember the frustration of driving through the Micmac—the congestion was so bad it even inspired a song. No one was able to capture the frustration quite the way Bryson Lyson did when they released "Micmac Rotary Blues" through Solar Records in 1982.

The song features a number of lyrical gems:

"I got up for work at seven, I figured I'd be there on time. But I didn't arrive 'til eleven—I should've been to work at nine."

"Five thousand people waitin' for their supper, they'd eat the soles right off your shoes. I've got the livin' in Dartmouth, workin' in Halifax Micmac Rotary blues."

There is also a Scottish folk dance called the Mic Mac Rotary which, based on YouTube listings, has been performed in both Scotland and Arkansas.

78

Sonic Youth played a (poorly attended) gig in the NSCAD cafeteria in 1984.

In 1984, just two years after Sonic Youth recorded their first EP, the Nova Scotia College of Art and Design (NSCAD) invited the iconic New York band to do a symposium in Halifax. The band took them up on the offer and on August 9, 1984, Thurston Moore, Kim Gordon, Lee Ranaldo, and their at-the-time drummer Bob Bert arrived at NSCAD with the sole purpose of speaking to one class.

When they were done, the band didn't have anything else to do, so they hung around, talked to some students, and made posters to advertise a gig they'd decided to play that evening. They plastered the school and the city with posters, but according to an interview with Moore, some Halifax feminists took exception and tore them down because one showed a woman being pulled into a grave by an undead hand.

Handmade posters for the last-minute Sonic Youth concert in Halifax in 1984. (Courtesy of Lee Ranaldo)

The poster tear-down, combined with the fact that there was a major punk show in the city that night, meant (according to Thurston Moore), there were only "about eight people" at a NSCAD cafeteria show that featured one of alternative rock's most influential bands.

79

Sons of Anarchy's Kim Coates lived in Halifax's Carleton Hotel and performed at Neptune Theatre in the 1980s.

Kim Coates is kind of a big deal. Not only has he had roles in movies like *Black Hawk Down*, *Hostage*, and *Silent Hill*, he's also a familiar face on television shows like *Entourage*, *CSI Miami*, *Prison Break*, and—most notably—*Sons of Anarchy*.

In the early 1980s, Neptune Theatre brought Coates to Halifax to perform in *West Side Story* and *Romeo and Juliet*. But according to Coates, the first Neptune play he performed in was *Ever Loving*. He spent three seasons in Halifax, performing in ten or eleven plays.

When he first arrived, he stayed in a Dartmouth hotel and took the ferry to rehearsals in Halifax but, as he told me in a 2013 interview, he "fell in love with the city," and decided to move into the Carleton Hotel on Argyle Street—now the Carleton Music Bar & Grill. He described his home at the hotel as "a shady little one-bedroom thing."

Coates is still able to rhyme off his favourite Halifax haunts. Most of them are gone now, but the classics include Bud the Spud, La Cave, the Misty Moon, the Press Gang, the Palace, and the Chickenburger.

80

North America's first tidal power plant opened on Hogg Island in 1984.

In 1984 the Annapolis Tidal Power Plant became the first tidal power plant in North America. Located on Hogg Island in the Annapolis River, the power plant was built by Nova Scotia Power (which was still owned by the Nova Scotia government at the time) as a pilot project to determine the viability of using the famous Fundy tides to generate electricity. The project started in 1980, and over the next four years the site was a flurry of activity as roads were rerouted, holes were dug, concrete was poured, the powerhouse was built, and turbines were installed. The end result was a station that generates around thirty gigawatt hours per year.

There are only three other major tidal power stations in the world—one in France, one in Russia, and one in South Korea. There's a good chance it's because tidal power plants can be detrimental to the environment.

The Annapolis Tidal Plant is one of only three of its kind in the world. Twice a day, as the tide changes, seawater is forced through the turbines to generate electricity.
(Joan Dawson)

According to Energy BC, between 20 and 80 percent of the fish that pass through a tidal barrage are killed. Since the Hogg Island power plant opened in 1984, there have been at least two incidents involving humpback whales. In 2004, a whale became trapped in the plant's basin for several days, and three years later the body of another humpback whale was found nearby.

81

The Tantallon coffee shop Train Station Bike & Bean was a functioning station until 1990.

Stroll, bike, or jog along the portion of Rails to Trails that winds through Tantallon and Head of Saint Margarets Bay, and you can't miss the bright orange caboose that still rests beside the old French Village Station. Built in 1904 by the Halifax and Southwestern Railway, the station is still in use today as a coffee and bike shop.

Step inside the station and chances are good you'll be walking into a bustling room full of conversation—but no one is waiting for trains anymore. The last freight train passed through the station in January 1990, on its way from Halifax to Yarmouth. Today, the building is set up with cozy tables, an acoustic playlist, walls full of local artwork, and a friendly barista or two. Walk through the café, and you'll find a room dedicated to cycling. If you're so inclined, you can rent a bike or buy some new gear.

There are still a few knick-knacks that remind visitors where they are: an old CN rail conductor's hat hangs on a hook near the coffee station, a framed list of stations hangs near the door, and a framed picture showing the French Village Station as it looked in the early 1900s. Back then, it was a different kind of community hub playing host to travellers who relied on a totally different kind of vehicle.

82

Mount Saint Vincent University started a lesbian pulp fiction collection in the 1990s.

In 1953, Gold Medal Books released *Spring Fire*, a book written by Marijane Meaker and published under the pseudonym Vin Packer. The novel told the tale of an inexperienced and unfortunate seventeen-year-old named Susan Mitchell (or Mitch, as she's called throughout the book), who falls in love with her college roommate, Leda. The book sold over three million copies and is considered the first true lesbian pulp fiction title. It's also part of Mount Saint Vincent University's 120-piece lesbian pulp fiction collection.

Mount Saint Vincent University professor Rhoda Zuk found most of the collection's books in Halifax bookstores during the early 1990s. According to Zuk, the collection is culturally and historically important because "many lesbians turned to this pulp fiction because it constituted their only source of affirmation of sexual identity."

The Mount's collection is used as a research and teaching resource in a number of its programs—everything from women's studies to psychology. And since most of the titles were written under pseudonyms, it's interesting to note that there are some well-known authors in the bunch. Marion Zimmer Bradley (*The Mists of Avalon*) used the pen names Miriam Gardner and Morgan Ives, while Lawrence Block (author of a long-running crime series featuring P. I. Matthew Scudder and "gentleman burglar" Bernie Rhodenbarr) wrote under the name Sheldon Lord.

83

Sloan's big break came in 1991 with a Battle of the Bands competition.

Canadian rock legends Sloan got their first big break in 1991 when they won a competition that landed them on a nineteen-track compilation put together by Dalhousie University's radio station, CKDU. *Hear and Now '92*, released by DTK Records of Fredericton, featured Sloan's song "Underwhelmed." And that's not all they got out of the competition: the band also won the chance to record with Terry Pulliam, one of the best producers in the region at the time.

When band members Jay Ferguson and Chris Murphy realized what this opportunity could mean for the band, they decided to pool their money so they could record enough songs to fill an album. The songs recorded in Pulliam's home studio were eventually used on the *Peppermint* EP, which the band released under its own label, Murderecords, in 1992.

Later that year, the band released its first full album, *Smeared*, with DGC Records. Even though Sloan had signed with another label, they continued to use Murderecords to support other local musicians, signing bands like Eric's Trip, Thrush Hermit, jale, The Inbreds, and The Super Friendz.

84

A Lunenburg farmer won the World's Strongest Man competition in 1992.

In 2014, *The Guinness Book of World Records* resurrected a category that had been noticeably absent for two decades: "The Greatest Weight Ever Lifted." The category had been dropped in 1984 when a record set by American weightlifter Paul Anderson was questioned because of difficulty in measuring his attempt. It seems that Guinness decided to err on the side of caution and removed the category entirely.

During that time, a Lunenburg famer named Gregg Ernst was competing in weightlifting competitions all over the world. In 1991, he lifted a pair of oxen at the South Shore Exhibition. The next year, he won the 1992 World's Strongest Man competition in Iceland by carrying the 418-pound Husafell Stone—a stone that's been used to test lifting strength for hundreds of years—for seventy metres. On July 28, 1993, he broke a world record when he achieved a lift of 5,340 pounds—in the form of two fully occupied Ford Festivas.

Even though Terry and Jan Todd, founders and co-directors of the H. J. Lutcher Stark Centre for Physical Culture and Sports, confirmed the record and Ernst had consulted with Guinness beforehand, the category wasn't reinstated when Ernst broke the record, and it didn't reappear until 2014. Even though Ernst is no longer entering weight lifting competitions, he finally has his name in *The Guinness Book of World Records.*

World's Strongest Man Gregg Ernst prepares to lift several thousand pounds of cinderblocks on his back in 1994. (Nova Scotia Archives)

85

Eleanor Johnson's 1992 thesis was the first to be written entirely in Mi'kmaw.

On May 11, 1992, Eleanor Johnson received her master's degree from Saint Mary's University in Halifax. Her thesis, titled "Mi'kmaq," was the first one ever written in Mi'kmaw from start to finish.

Johnson's thesis addressed the fundamentals of "tribal consciousness as an enduring paradigm for living that is still employed by the Mi'kmaq people," and looked at a number of specific values that have helped the Mi'kmaq people survive without sacrificing their world view—things like family life, belief systems, and medicine. These values include respect for elders, man, and nature, and an appreciation for sharing and cooperation.

Johnson's abstract also clarifies that although non-Mi'kmaw scholars have examined tribal consciousness in the past, their research and reporting was inadequate. Johnson wanted to rectify the lack of accurate information.

After interviewing a number of elders living in Cape Breton, she began writing her thesis entirely in Mi'kmaw in an effort to more accurately capture the concept of tribal consciousness. Because the structure of the Mi'kmaw language is fundamentally different than English—focusing on verbs instead of nouns and, as Johnson writes, emphasizing "relationships and states of being rather than things"—her language choice made it possible to create a unique thesis that reflects the concept of tribal consciousness in a deeper way.

86

Robert Munsch's book *Lighthouse* was inspired by his 1993 visit to Antigonish.

Lighthouse: A Story of Remembrance tells the story of a young girl named Sarah who has just lost her grandfather. Unable to sleep, she asks her father to take her on a moonlit adventure to visit the lighthouse she and Grandpa used to visit together.

Robert Munsch, author of classic picture books like *Love You Forever*, *Murmel Murmel Murmel*, and *The Paper Bag Princess*, was inspired to write *Lighthouse* in 1993, after reading at a theatre in Antigonish. Before he left the theatre, he discovered that a child named Sarah Gillis had left him a gift—a drawing of a lighthouse. He spent the whole drive to his next reading drafting the story that would eventually become *Lighthouse*. With help from the staff at the Antigonish Library, Munsch was able to figure out who the artist was and mail her his story.

When Scholastic decided to publish the book in 2001, Munsch reached out to Gillis again. Gillis took some time to show him around Antigonish and tell him about her childhood there. They toured the Cape George Lighthouse in Antigonish County, as well as Mabou, where Gillis's grandmother lived. They took plenty of photos along the way, and illustrator Janet Wilson drew heavily on those photos for the book, creating an ambience that's pure Nova Scotia.

The cover of Lighthouse: A Story of Remembrance, *originally published in 2003. (Reproduced by permission of Scholastic Canada Ltd.)*

87

The Pugwash Conference on Science and World Affairs won the Nobel Peace Prize in 1995.

On July 9, 1955, Bertrand Russell read a statement to a group of London reporters. Co-written by Albert Einstein and signed by nine other prominent scientists, the Russell–Einstein Manifesto outlined the destructive potential of atomic weapons. Its writers called for a conference where the great scientific minds of the time could set aside their individual agendas and discuss the implications of atomic war.

An excerpt from the manifesto states, "In view of the fact that in any future world war nuclear weapons will certainly be employed, and that such weapons threaten the continued existence of mankind, we urge the governments of the world to realize, and to acknowledge publicly, that their purpose cannot be furthered by a world war, and we urge them, consequently, to find peaceful means for the settlement of all matters of dispute between them."

Two years later, the dream was realized when Cyrus Eaton, an investment banker who owned a summer home in Pugwash, offered to fund the conference as long as they agreed to hold it at his summer home—now a Canadian National Historic Site known as Thinkers Lodge. The result was the first Pugwash Conference on Science and World Affairs, titled "Appraisal of Dangers from Atomic Weapons."

That first meeting drew twenty-two scientists from all over the world, including E. H. S. Burhop, D. F. Cavers, J. S. Foster, Mark Oliphant, and Joseph Rotblat. Unfortunately, Einstein had passed away and Russell became too ill to travel before the first conference. Since then, there have been more than four hundred meetings.

In 1995, Joseph Rotblat, who served as president of the conference from 1988 to 1997, and the Pugwash Conference on Science and World Affairs were jointly awarded the Nobel Peace Prize for their efforts to reduce the use of (and eventually eliminate) nuclear arms.

88

A 1998 song by Halifax band Plumtree inspired the *Scott Pilgrim* graphic novels.

In 2010, a full decade after the Halifax band Plumtree split up, they experienced a new surge in popularity. Their 1998 song "Scott Pilgrim," which featured the repeated angsty lyrics "I've liked you for a thousand years," inspired the name of Bryan Lee O'Malley's protagonist and trademark graphic novel series. And in 2010, that series spawned a movie.

Scott Pilgrim vs. the World, featuring a geeky namesake protagonist (Michael Cera) and love interest Ramona Flowers (Mary Elizabeth Winstead) is a nod-heavy homage to classic video games and indie rock. As Pilgrim fights his way through a progressively difficult series of Flowers's "evil exes," astute viewers will notice a number of band references, from Pilgrim's yellow and red Plumtree T-shirt to the posters of Plumtree song titles.

In an interview on Fluxblog, Bryan Lee O'Malley said, "I thought about their song and, you know, who is this guy Scott Pilgrim anyway, and what's so great about him? And like I was saying, we were riding the bus and talking about Scott Pilgrim, and a bunch of the crazy stuff we came up with ended up being some of the basis for his character and his sort of world view."

Plumtree's Carla Gillis wrote in a 2010 article for *The Coast*, "There had been an attempt to record with Philip Pilgrim, a music producer friend of a friend...The song title came from Scott Ingram, chartered accountant to the (indie rock) stars...Lynette was telling a story about Scott Ingram and mixed him up with Philip Pilgrim and when the two names collided, we laughed 'til we got giddy."

89

A Nova Scotia fisherman had a close encounter with an eight-foot-long "sea serpent" in 2003.

In June 2003, a Cape Breton lobster fisherman named Wallace Cartwright had a rather unusual afternoon. He was headed into a cove near the Point Aconi lighthouse with his sternman when he saw what looked like a large log—until he caught sight of a head and the "log" rose about a foot out of the water before submerging again as the boat approached.

Cartwright followed the creature—which he described as smooth, brown, three to four hundred pounds, and about eight feet long—for about forty-five minutes, before it headed towards deeper water.

Although there's no way to confirm exactly what the creature was without an actual specimen, Andrew Hebda, curator of zoology at the Nova Scotia Museum of Natural History, thinks it was an oarfish. This species of fish has four subspecies, one of which is the giant oarfish or "king of herrings." They're considered the largest known living species of bony fish and can grow up to fifty-six feet long and weigh as much as six hundred pounds.

Oarfish have been the culprits behind many "sea serpent" sightings over the last couple of centuries, and they've even worked their way into Japanese folklore: the story goes that when a large number of slender oarfish (another of the four subspecies) wash up on shore, an earthquake is on the way.

90

In 2003, a 125-year-old church was sailed to a new home across Bras d'Or Lake.

Malagawatch United Church was over 125 years old when it was taken off its foundation and moved to a new home at the Highland Village in Iona. The church, originally consecrated in 1874, was built in response to a growing community which had outgrown its existing Presbyterian church.

By 2003, however, the church had fallen into disuse. It was no longer being used for regular services, and its remaining parishioners decided to sell it to the Highland Village Museum—which had been hoping to add a church to its site for a long time.

On Tuesday, November 25, 2003, the 2,000-square-foot church was taken off its foundation and moved a kilometre and a half down Marble Mountain Road, towards the River Denys Basin and the barge that would

The Malagawatch United Church floating down Bras d'Or Lake on a barge in 2007. (Courtesy of SuperPort Marine Services)

carry it across the Bras d'Or Lake. It took some time to load it onto the barge, but by mid-afternoon the church set sail for Iona to the applause of about three hundred onlookers.

Two hours and fifteen nautical miles later, it arrived in the Barra Strait, where it waited for the right tides to carry it safely through the bridges. Finally, after a full day, the church was tied to a wharf in Iona, where it waited overnight. It took a couple of days to get it ready for the last leg of its journey—from the wharf, down Highway 223, and up the steep hill to the Highland Village Museum.

There must have been a few white-knuckle moments as the church moved up the hill, but around 9:15 P.M. on Friday, November 28, it finally reached its destination. The Malagawatch United Church eventually got a new foundation, an extensive restoration, and its original steeple. The whole project cost $300,000.

91

In 2005, the Department of Natural Resources caught eight poachers using mechanical moose.

There are fewer than one thousand mainland moose left in Nova Scotia, thanks to a combination of disease, poaching, predatory kills, and disturbed habitat. In 2003, this species of moose was declared endangered. Unfortunately, when the declaration was made, not everyone listened. That same year, hunters illegally killed three moose in the Sherbrooke area.

The killings prompted Nova Scotia's Department of Natural Resources to launch Operation Crossroad, a sting operation that used high-tech, realistic, mechanical moose decoys to catch poachers. For two years, twelve Natural Resources officers looked into complaints about suspected poachers and then hid in blinds, watching the mechanical decoys in action.

Their work began to pay off when a hunter from Pugwash shot the first decoy—a mechanical moose nicknamed "Bullwinkle." Under the Endangered Species Act, the penalty for shooting at an endangered animal can reach up to $500,000 or a six-month prison sentence. The man who shot Bullwinkle lost his hunting license, his car, his rifle, and about $4,025.

In late 2005, eight more individuals appeared in court on charges of killing endangered mainland moose. Two of those people were a father–son hunting team who, according to their defense lawyer, fired at Bullwinkle out of "hunter's instinct." They were each fined $8,100 and lost their hunting licenses and guns.

92

Halifax Stanfield International Airport was an emergency landing site for the space shuttle Discovery in 2006.

On July 4, 2006, the space shuttle Discovery took off from the Kennedy Space Center in Florida with seven people on board: Commander Steven W. Lindsey, pilot Mark E. Kelly, and mission specialists Stephanie D. Wilson, Michael E. Fossum, Piers J. Sellers, Thomas Reiter, and Lisa M. Nowak.

Before the launch, NASA designated Halifax International Airport one of five space shuttle emergency landing sites in Atlantic Canada—the others were at airports in Newfoundland. These sites were put in place in case anything went wrong after takeoff, or if the shuttle needed a quick place to land any time during the mission. The astronauts even used a simulator to practice an emergency Halifax landing.

According to an article in the July 5, 2006, edition of the *Chronicle-Herald*, the chance of Discovery making an emergency landing in Nova Scotia was about 1 percent, but if it were to happen, people all over Nova Scotia would hear multiple sonic booms.

The Discovery crew got a lot done during their 2006 mission—they tested and inspected the Discovery's thermal protection system, replaced important hardware, and left Thomas Reiter behind to help man the International Space Station until he could join another mission. They also left behind a new heat exchanger, a new window and window seals for the Microgravity Sciences Glovebox, a US extravehicular activity suit, and a jet pack.

All went as planned, and the shuttle landed safely back on Earth on July 17, 2006—twelve days, eighteen hours, thirty-seven minutes, and fifty-four seconds after takeoff.

93

Nova Scotia was the first jurisdiction in North America to make LED streetlights mandatory in 2011.

In April 2009, the ecoNova Scotia Fund for Clean Air and Climate Change and Conserve Nova Scotia teamed up to provide funding to replace high-pressure sodium lights with 1,100 LED streetlights throughout the province. The deal was struck with a company called LED Roadway Lighting, which is based in Halifax but does its primary manufacturing in Amherst. Annapolis Royal was the first town to benefit from the funding. When the 1,100 lights were installed in October 2009, it became the first town in North America to be completely refitted with LED streetlights.

On April 21, 2011, the Nova Scotia government announced legislation which made LED street lighting mandatory. According to a government press release, the legislation aimed to reduce energy costs and lower both greenhouse gas and mercury emissions. Municipalities across the province and Nova Scotia Power were given five years to complete the transition.

The *Chronicle-Herald* published an article in April 2014 under the headline "Halifax to buy street lights from Nova Scotia Power." The article stated that "up to eighteen municipalities, including New Minas and Digby, are also negotiating to buy street lights from Nova Scotia Power before switching the lights to energy-saving LEDs." Halifax, on the other hand, is currently still on the fence. According to a May 21, 2015, *Chronicle-Herald* article, the switch is estimated to cost about $47 million, which is $7 million more than originally anticipated.

94

In 2011, Bill Clinton gave a keynote speech at St. Francis Xavier University in Antigonish.

When the Nova Scotia university officially opened the Frank McKenna Centre for Leadership on May 11, 2011, it celebrated with a gala that attracted more than six hundred people. The cost to attend was $150 a plate, and the two keynote speakers were former New Brunswick premier Frank McKenna—who donated $1 million of the $10 million required to open the centre—and former US president Bill Clinton who, according to *the Globe and Mail*, is pretty good friends with McKenna.

During his keynote speech, Clinton spoke about Haiti, which was still reeling from the devastating 2010 earthquake and subsequent tsunamis that forced about 1.5 million people from their homes. He talked about the level of leadership that was required for Haiti to successfully rebuild and went on to say that he thinks "many of the world's challenges in the twenty-first century will require unique partnerships between government, business, and non-governmental groups."

Finally, he praised the new centre, saying, "If you have a great university, even if it's in a small town in Nova Scotia, it can reach across the world to lift up all kinds of people."

95

The two youngest people to discover supernovas (in 2011 and 2013) are from the same Nova Scotia family.

Dave Lane is a systems administrator at Saint Mary's University's Department of Astronomy and Physics, and the director of the school's Burke-Gaffney Observatory. He's also the owner of the Abbey Ridge Observatory in Stillwater Lake, where a number of notable astronomical discoveries have been made.

Lane's first big discovery was made in the Burke-Gaffney Observatory in February 1995, when he co-discovered a supernova with Paul Gray—making them the first two Canadians to discover a supernova on home soil. On January 11, 2005, a photo taken at the semi-automated Abbey Ridge Observatory triggered the second big discovery made by the Gray–Lane team: another supernova in the observatory's images.

On January 2, 2011, discovery of supernovas became a family affair when Gray's then ten-year-old daughter, Kathryn Aurora Gray, discovered a supernova in images from the Abbey Ridge Observatory, making her the youngest person (at the time) to co-discover a catastrophic astronomical event. She was rewarded with the opportunity to meet Neil Armstrong, a letter of recognition from the prime minister, and a pound of Canadian back bacon from her father's astronomy club.

Kathryn's brother, Nathan Gray, beat her record on October 30, 2013, when he and Lane co-discovered a supernova in the Draco constellation. Just thirty-three days younger than Kathryn was when she made her discovery, Nathan found his supernova while digging through images from his home in Greenwood, Nova Scotia, while his sister was out.

96

Nova Scotia didn't repeal the waiting period for marriage licenses until 2013.

There was a lot going on in Nova Scotia in 1931. The minister of health was trying to figure out how to control tuberculosis outbreaks in Cape Breton, almost 20 percent of the province's wage-earning population was out of work, Christie's Restaurant in Sydney was selling full-course chicken dinners for just fifty cents, and the government added a mandatory waiting period to the Solemnization of Marriage Act.

If you wanted to get married in Nova Scotia in 1931, you had to apply and then wait five days before you could pick up the license granting you permission to wed. In its early days, this waiting period gave the issuer of the license time to ensure that couples applying to marry had completed all the requirements, and that there weren't any legal issues that could impede the marriage. There were exceptions, of course. If the applicants had a good reason, the issuer had the power to waive the waiting period and issue the license for a fee of five dollars.

Over the years, Canadian provinces slowly repealed their waiting periods, but Nova Scotia held on until the bitter end. On May 10, 2013, Service Nova Scotia Minister John MacDonell announced that the government was eliminating the requirement. In a press release, he stated, "We are responding to Nova Scotians' need to have efficient and convenient access to government services while respecting that adults do not require a government-forced period to think about their marriage."

97

In 2014, an eighty-five-year-old time capsule was discovered in a Kentville high school.

On June 19, 1929, a small lead box was placed in a hollowed-out granite block that served as the cornerstone for the Kings County Academy, the new senior high school that had recently been built in Kentville for eight hundred dollars.

Dr. H. F. Munro, superintendent of education, laid the cornerstone, but it seems that he—or someone else in the administration—wanted to commemorate the opening of the school with more than just an inscription.

In 2001, the Kings County Academy was decommissioned, and students were moved to the nearby Northeast Kings Education Centre. The school was finally demolished in May 2014, almost eighty-five years after it was constructed. During the demolition, workers found the lead box hidden in the cornerstone.

To avoid damage, the time capsule was taken to a lab to be unpacked, and the following artifacts were uncovered:

- A seven-page document that described Kentville school history, including its curriculum and faculty
- Three newspapers, two dated June 19, 1929 (the *Halifax Herald* and the *Halifax Chronicle*), and one dated April 18, 1929 (*The Advertiser*)
- Two business cards: one from the Dominion Atlantic Railway, and one from Harry Morse, the town clerk and treasurer.

98

Nova Scotia has been producing world-recognized actors since the early 1900s

Whether you're driving through Lunenburg or Halifax, it's not uncommon to see cryptic yellow signs, hand-lettered with thick black marker, stapled to power poles or attached to stakes. These signs point the way to filming locations, so if you happen to see one, chances are you're getting close to a film set.

In the recent past, this was Nova Scotia's movie-related claim to fame: it's a great place to film. What people don't know is how many successful actors have come out of the province. Famous Nova Scotian actors include:

- Craig Olejnik (*Thirteen Ghosts*)
- John Reardon (TRON: *Legacy*)
- Leslie Hope (*Never Back Down*)
- Peter Donat (*The Godfather Part II*)
- Ellen Page (*Juno, Inception*)
- David Manners (*Dracula*)
- Cindy Sampson (*The Shrine*)
- Glen Matthews (*Hobo With a Shotgun*)
- Liam McNamara (*Outlander*)
- Troy Veinotte (*The Hanging Garden*)
- Joseph Lee (*Transformers*)

99

The Tides of History theatre at the Citadel Hill National Historic Site is haunted.

According to Harold R. Thompson, writer and Parks Canada staff member, some strange things have been reported at Citadel Hill's Tides of History display. In *Ghosts and Folklore of the Halifax Citadel National Site,* he tells the stories of three co-workers who have had unsettling experiences while working near the display. The Tides of History featured four theatres that combine to explain the history of the Citadel using a combination of projected slides and actual artifacts.

Some staff members have simply felt "an eerie presence" in the area, particularly in Theatre 4, while others have spookier experiences. One employee heard her name whispered while she was getting ready to vacuum, and another saw the gray outline of a man appear on the security monitor for Theatre 2 but couldn't find anyone anywhere near the area. A third saw a man shuffling the papers on display in Theatre 4, but was unable to find him. A fourth witnessed a similar occurrence in Theatre 3.

After hearing the stories, Thompson and a co-worker decided to find out whether it's possible to enter and exit the area without anyone seeing or hearing. Thompson pretended to be an attendant, and his co-worker played the part of the "intruder." They tried three times, and Thompson caught his colleague red-handed twice. The third time, he could hear her footsteps as she ran away. Although Thompson admits that this was by no means a scientific test, it still makes you wonder what secrets the Tides of History display really holds.

高沙查.
1万5千公顷的社区森林.

100

There are over 15,000 hectares of community forest in Nova Scotia

Currently, there are more than one hundred community forests across Canada, but most of them are in British Columbia, Ontario, and Quebec. In late 2013, however, the Nova Scotia government announced that it was negotiating a three-year Crown forest agreement with a for-profit organization called Medway Community Forest Co-operative. The project was prompted by a few factors, including the province's dwindling pulp industry, and the thinning old-growth forest. The idea was that a community forest would offer local residents control over their own economic opportunities, without having to go too far from home.

Community forests are collaborative projects that make it easier for people who live near them to maximize the economic, ecological, and sociological benefits. According to "Advancing the Conversation on Community Forests in Nova Scotia: Proceedings from the June 2012 Forum on Community Forests" by L. Kris MacLellan and Peter N. Duinker:

> Community forests create a great diversity of types of employment and skills development programs, as well as tending to attract labourers who might not be employed in the traditional workforce. Community forests foster openness to partnerships and synergy with local groups, relying in some ways on the natural openness to partnerships that is traditionally found in non-profit groups.

Today, the Medway Community Forest Co-operative—which is supported by a number of groups including Windhorse Woods, the Federation of Nova Scotia Woodland Owners and Operators Association, and the Ecology Action Centre—controls fifteen thousand hectares of Crown land in Annapolis County. In late 2014, the Nova Scotia government awarded $274,000 to the project, and the final agreement, which supports a three-year pilot project, was signed on January 30, 2015.

Epilogue

Whenever someone asks me about this book or "50 Things You Don't Know About Halifax," the first question is usually "How do you find so many things?" And quite honestly, the challenge isn't finding the things—it's narrowing them down. One of the biggest things I learned throughout this process is that when it comes to historical research, the more you dig, the more you discover, and the more you discover, the more you dig... until suddenly it's 11:30 P.M. and you're reading about the walruses on Sable Island. The real challenge in writing something like this is finding the context and the details surrounding these facts, because so much gets lost over time.

Nova Scotia is a fascinating province with a rich history, and there's a lot to discover if you know where to look. Whether you live in Nova Scotia or an entirely different part of the country, if you want to know more about the place you call home, start at your local library. Visit your municipal archives. Dig through old newspapers and read the plaques in national parks. Look up the old street names. But more than anything, talk to people. Talk to your taxi driver and your bartender, your neighbour and your great-aunt. Everyone has stories to share, so go forth and discover! Then start a blog or a Twitter account, write a book, or just go out and tell your own stories to someone else.

Because the more stories we share, the richer our collective history becomes.

Text Sources

Akins, Thomas Beamish. *Selections from the Public Documents of the Province of Nova Scotia*. Halifax: Charles Annand, 1869, 585–90.

———. *History of Halifax City: Illustrated with Maps and Engravings*. Belleville, Ontario: Mika Publishing Company, 1973, 158.

Appleton, Thomas E. "History of the Canadian Coast Guard and Marine Services." Government of Canada: Fisheries and Oceans Canada, 2013.

Barclay, Michael, Ian A. D. Jack, and Jason Schneider. *Have Not Been the Same: The CanRock Renaissance, 1985-1995*. Toronto: ECW Press, 2011.

Baylaucq, Philippe. *Moving Sands*, Productions La Fête (Sable) Inc., 2003. DVD.

Berwick, Aaron. "Leon Trotsky Forged Notable Month at Amherst Foundry-turned Internment Camp," *The Chronicle-Herald*, January 2, 2015.

Boileau, John. "Storm of the Century," *Saltscapes Magazine*, January/February 2005.

Brookes, Ann. "Oscar Wilde and the Aesthetic Movement," *Cranleigh Decorative & Fine Arts Society*, 2011.

Buggey, Susan. "Biography: Downs, Andrew," vol. 12, 1891–1900, *Dictionary of Canadian Biography*, n.d.

Butler, Erica. "So Near, Yet so Far," *Halifax Magazine*, July 2014.

Canadian Broadcasting Corporation. "Hockey: A People's History—Episode 1: A Simple Game." CBC/Radio Canada (website), n.d.

Cane, Ryan. "A Lesson in History," *Hockey Canada*. January 4, 2003.

Carvery, Irvine. *The History of Africville As Told by the People of Africville*, Ottawa: Library and Archives Canada. 2008.

"Cheers!: Eastern Canada's 19th Century Brewery and Distillery Industry," *Canada's Historic Places* (website), n.d.

Christie, Marion. "Growing up in Bedford 1914–1930," *Community Memories*, Virtual Museum of Canada, 2013.

Delefes, Peter. "Harold R. Foster—Creator of the Prince Valiant Adventure Comic Strip," *The Griffin*, vol. 37.3. Halifax: Heritage Trust of Nova Scotia, 2012.

Dunlop, Allan C. "Biography: Fraser, James Daniel Bain," vol. 9, 1861–1870, *Dictionary of Canadian Biography*, n.d.

Elliott, Wendy. "Ghost Islands of Nova Scotia," *Kings County Register*, April 27, 2012.

Flinn, Sue Carter. "NSCAD: Where Art and Music Converge," *The Coast*, September 3, 2009.

"From Chloroform To Epidurals: New Book By UF Physician Examines History Of Labor Pain Relief." *ScienceDaily* (website), March 1, 2000.

Geere, Duncan. "How the First Cable Was Laid across the Atlantic," *Wired UK*, January 18, 2011.

Gillis, Carla. "Pilgrim and a Plumtree," *The Coast*, August 12, 2010.

Gooding, Christopher. "Book of Negroes Series Re-connects Amherst to 'The Rock,'" *Amherst News*, February 4, 2015.

Government of Nova Scotia. *Legislative Changes Take Some of the Stress out of Getting Married.* April 3, 2013.

Grant, John N. "Black Immigrants into Nova Scotia, 1776–1815," *The Journal of Negro History*. 1973, 253–70.

Helston, Charlotte. "Overview," *EnergyBC: Tidal Power* (website), n.d.

Hewson, John. "Introduction to Micmac Hieroglyphics," *Cape Breton's Magazine*, January 1988, 55.

Hillmer, Norman. "Silver Dart," *Historica Canada* (website), July 2006.

"Historical Account of the Courts," *History of the Court of Chancery in Nova Scotia*, n.d.

"Highway Driving Rule Changes Sides." *Automobiles: The Early Days in NS* (website), n.p., n.d.

"Ice Skates—Starr Manufacturing Company." *Nova Scotia Museum* (website), April 23, 2013.

Jobb, Dean. *The Cajuns: A People's Story of Exile and Triumph.* New York, New York: John Wiley & Sons, 2005.

Kane, Brian. "Hal Foster," JVJ Publishing, n.d.

Kelly, Gemey. *Arthur Lismer: Nova Scotia, 1916–1919*. Halifax: Dalhousie Art Gallery, 1982.

Lambie, Chris. "Halifax Possible Shuttle Pit Stop; Airport on Crew's List of Emergency Landing Sites." *The Chronicle-Herald,* July 5, 2006.

Macdonald, Clyde F. *Murder Cases in Pictou County: 1811-1950.* New Glasgow, Nova Scotia: Clyde F. MacDonald, 2006.

MacLeod, Ken. "Bring Your Best Singing Voice," *Cape Breton Post*, December 23, 2012.

McCarthy, Brendan, and the Nova Scotia Sport Hall of Fame. "Remembering Babe Ruth's Trip to Halifax in '42," *On the Go*, vol. 5.1, 2012.

"Marine Heritage Database," *On the Rocks: Shipwrecks of Nova Scotia*, Halifax: Maritime Museum of the Atlantic, n.d.

Marsh, James H. "Joseph Howe: Tribune of Nova Scotia," *The Canadian Encyclopedia* (website), February 1, 2011.

Matheson, Trueman. *A History of Londonderry, Nova Scotia*. Londonderry, Nova Scotia: Trueman Matheson, 1989.

Murdoch, Beamish. "Appendix to Chapter XI," *A History of Nova-Scotia or Acadie*. Halifax: James Barnes, 1866, 147–51.

Newton, Pamela. *The Cape Breton Book of Days*. Sydney, Nova Scotia: Cape Breton University Press, 2005.

Njeru, Purity. "History of Freetown," *The African Executive*, March 21, 2007.

O'Connor, D'Arcy. *The Secret Treasure of Oak Island: The Amazing True Story of a Centuries-old Treasure Hunt*. Guilford, Connecticut: Lyons, 2004.

Oxner, Cliff, and Ruth Oxner. *Chester Basin Memories, 1749–1989*. Chester Basin, Nova Scotia: Cliff Oxner, 1989.

Pallotta, Frank. "How Dwayne 'The Rock' Johnson Went From WWE Wrestler To Hollywood's Box Office Champ," *Business Insider*, July 2014.

Pedwell, Terry. "Canadian Museum of History Pays $300,000 to Nova Scotia Man for World's Oldest Known Hockey Stick," *The National Post*, January 9, 2015.

"Province Makes It Easier To Get Hitched," *The Huffington Post*, March 4, 2013.

"Quaternary Period, Quaternary Period Information, Prehistoric Facts," *National Geographic* (website), n.d.

Semhar, Negassa. "Freetown, Sierra Leone (1792–)," *The Black Past: Remembered and Reclaimed* (website), n.d.

Tattrie, Jon. "Africville," *The Canadian Encyclopedia* (website), January 27, 2014.

———. *The Hermit of Africville: The Life of Eddie Carvery*. East Lawrencetown, Nova Scotia: Pottersfield Press, 2010.

Taylor, Wanda. *Still Here: A Journey to Triumph*, directed by Wanda Taylor (YouTube), January 8, 2015.

Thompson, Harold R. *Ghosts and Folklore of the Halifax Citadel National Historic Site*. Halifax: Harold R. Thompson, 2005.

"University Receives Final Editions of Gaelic Newspaper." *Herald Scotland*, June 29, 1997.

Windsor, Hillary, and Mark Gillis. "Prisons of Halifax's past," *Halifacts* (blog), November 25, 2014.

Winthrop, John, and James Savage. *The History of New England from 1630 to 1649*. Boston: Little, Brown, 1853.

Zentilli, Marcos. "Geological Notes." *Backlands Coalition* (website), April 1, 2014.